Hymns that Endure

Hymns
THAT
Endure

W. THORBURN CLARK

Late Pastor and Author of
Outriders for the King,
Handmaidens of the King,
Trophies for the King, and
Stories of Fadeless Hymns

BROADMAN PRESS | Nashville, Tennessee

© 1942 · Broadman Press

Nashville, Tennessee

422-07201

Library of Congress catalog card number: 42-24853

Printed in the United States of America

7.5JE6013

To

MY WIFE

Whose Untiring Labors
and
Sympathetic Criticisms
Have Aided in the Preparation
of These and Other Pages

THIS BOOK

IS

AFFECTIONATELY DEDICATED

CONTENTS

PREFACE

Although a number of excellent books of hymn stories have been written, nevertheless, I feel that the following pages may find a place of their own, and perform a helpful mission.

In dealing with a hymn and its story, it is my plan to give a brief biography of the author, the circumstances under which it was written, and instances of its use.

Not only do the sentiments of the hymns mentioned enrich the thoughts and ennoble the actions of those who familiarize themselves with them, but the lives of the writers also become an inspiration, for they reveal the depths of consecrated living from which came these exalted compositions.

I hope that this book may be helpful to Christian workers in various spheres of activity; to the minister in announcing his hymns; to the chorister in selecting the music; to the superintendent of the Sunday school, to the leaders of prayer meetings, of missionary groups, and of young people's gatherings in preparing the musical part of their programs. And may it find a place in the devotional reading of the home, deepening its spiritual life.

I wish to express my sincere appreciation to the following who have generously given me the privilege of using material from their own publications: Philip E. Howard, Jr., associate editor of *The Sunday School Times;* Dr. Delavan L. Pierson, editor of *The Missionary Review of the World;* George T. B. Davis, author of *Twice Around the World with Alexander;* Allan Sutherland, author of *Famous*

Hymns of the World; D. J. Paine for the use of incidents from *Stories of the Great Hymns of the Church,* by Silas H. Paine; Funk and Wagnalls Company for quotations from *The Homiletic Review,* from *English Hymns and Their Authors,* by Dr. Samuel Willoughby Duffield, and from *Followers of the Gleam,* by Dr. Charles L. Goodell; Fleming H. Revell Company for material from *Down in Water Street,* by Samuel H. Hadley, from *Recollections of a Long Life,* by Dr. Theodore L. Cuyler, and from *Fanny Crosby's Story of Ninety-four Years,* by S. Travena Jackson; the American Tract Society for the use of incidents from *The Story of the Hymns and Tunes,* by Theron Brown and Hezekiah Butterworth, and from the proceedings of the Ecumenical Missionary Conference, New York, 1900; Mrs. Margaret C. Munns, chairman, Publishing Committee, National W.C.T.U., for the privilege of using quotations from *Glimpses of Fifty Years,* by Frances E. Willard, and from *The Beautiful Life of Frances E. Willard,* by Anna A. Gordon.

I appreciate the incident on "When I Survey the Wondrous Cross," furnished at my request by Dr. J. W. Storer, pastor of the First Baptist Church of Tulsa, Oklahoma.

Several of these chapters appeared in *The Teacher,* published by The Sunday School Board of the Southern Baptist Convention, and I esteem the privilege, given by Dr. Hight C Moore, editorial secretary, of including them in this volume.

Among other books that I have found informative and stimulating in these studies are: *Annotations Upon Popular Hymns,* by Dr. Charles Seymour Robinson; *The Romance of Sacred Song,* by David J. Beattie; *Hymns in Human Experience,* by Dr. William J. Hart; *Hymns, Historically Famous,* by

Colonel Nicholas Smith; *The Hymn as Literature,* by Dr. Jeremiah Bascom Reeves; *Baptist Hymn Writers and Their Hymns,* by Dr. Henry S. Burrage; *Story of the Gospel Hymns,* by Ira D. Sankey; *Memorials of Frances Ridley Havergal,* by Maria V. G. Havergal; and *The Wonderful Career of Moody and Sankey,* by Dr. E. J. Goodspeed.

May these stories of HYMNS THAT ENDURE be a source of information, enjoyment, and inspiration to the reader, and bring honor to the name of him for whose glory these great hymns were written.

Richmond, Virginia
1942

—W. THORBURN CLARK

INTRODUCTION

Of incalculable value to the presentation of the gospel have been the hymns that we sing as Christian worshipers. These great hymns have come down to us through the years, gathering a company of new messages and messengers as they have traveled. Through them the gospel message has been vocal for uncounted thousands. To many of them has been attached a sentimental reverie that has sustained in times of stress.

Hymns endure—and it is well that there are those who have the patience and interest to search out their history, and inscribe their biographies. There is value in such a record. It will help us to appreciate with a new distinction the place of music in our religious expression. It will help us to vitalize our extension of this religion to others. It will make more personal the message the hymn itself has for each heart.

Such a contribution, the author has made in this volume. Out of a long and fruitful ministry he reaps the scholarly associations he has known with these hymns, and makes them living forces worthy of perpetuation. The name of W. Thorburn Clark is linked with the personal development of the religious experience of many who like myself made a profession of faith under his preaching, and who through the years have felt the impact of his godliness—a ripe spiritual influence for his Master. He continues his ministry through his pen to bless even more than he has touched with his preached word.

—C. SYLVESTER GREEN
President, Coker College

Hartsville, South Carolina.

I

ABIDE WITH ME

Frances Ridley Havergal, whose hymns have brought inspiration to a multitude of hearts, was spending a short while in Switzerland in 1874. One evening she climbed to a point on one of the mountains, from which she had a magnificent view of the valley beneath and the mountain peaks above her. For a long time she gazed upon the panorama of hills and clouds before her, hills immovable, but clouds ever changing their color and shape.

Miss Havergal says: "At one juncture a cloud stood still, apparently about two hundred yards off, and we each saw our own shadows gigantically reflected in it, surrounded by a complete rainbow arch, but a full circle of bright prismatic colors, a transfiguration of our shadows almost startling."

Then as the magnificent pageant faded, and the evening shadows began to fall about them, she and her companions joined in singing,

> Abide with me, fast falls the eventide;
> The darkness deepens; Lord, with me abide.

"Abide With Me," was written by Henry F. Lyte, who was born at Kelso, Scotland, on June 1, 1793.

As a youth he was a diligent student, and after attending preparatory school he went to Trinity College, Dublin, and three times during his college course he received a prize for English poetry. His family were in moderate circumstances, and the amount of these prizes was of great assistance to him in meeting his financial needs while pursuing his studies. At first he expected to become a physician, but finally decided against this profession, and entered the ministry of the Episcopal Church.

He was ordained in 1815. At this time he did not seem to have any special religious conviction, but in 1818 he was summoned to the deathbed of a neighboring clergyman, who, like himself, had had no deep spiritual experience. As they communed together in this trying hour they came to a consecration to which they previously had been strangers, —one to be sustained by his new-found faith, as he soon departed to be forever with his Lord, the other to be kept in fellowship with his Saviour through years of devoted service on earth.

In relating this incident, Mr. Lyte says of his friend: "He died happy under the belief that, though he had deeply erred, there was One whose death and sufferings would atone for his delinquences, and be accepted for all that he had incurred." And he added: "I was greatly affected by the whole matter, and brought to look at life and its issue with a different eye than before; and I began to study my Bible and preach in another manner than I had previously done."

Mr. Lyte's first parish was near the town of Wexford. Some years later, in 1823, he took up his residence at Lower Brixam, Devonshire, England, and this was his home during the rest of his life. He married the daughter of Rev. W. Maxwell, D.D., of Bath.

At Brixam, he came in contact with the rough fishermen of the sea, soldiers from the barracks, and visitors who came for the benefit of bathing in the salt water. To all, rich and poor, he ministered with a sacrificial devotion.

Mr. Lyte had the unique distinction of living in an elegant home presented to him by his king, William IV, who, when he visited the town, was met by Mr. Lyte, accompanied by a surpliced choir. The monarch was so impressed by this reception, and by the genuine courtesies shown him by the Brixam clergyman, that he made him a gift of this beautiful residence. Here Mr. Lyte lived for nearly twenty-five years, preaching, studying, ministering to the wants of his people, and writing his immortal hymns. "Jesus, I My Cross Have Taken," is one of his popular productions.

For years the poet suffered from tuberculosis, and the dread malady baffled the best skill of the medical profession. His health steadily declined, and in the autumn of 1847 his physicians advised him to give up his work at Brixam and spend the winter in Italy. On the last Sunday of his stay in England he preached a tender farewell sermon, and administered the Lord's Supper. It was a tearful occasion for both minister and congregation.

Some years before this, feeling that his journey through this life would not be long extended, and desiring to write something that would live after him for the glory of his Lord, he penned these lines:

> Might verse of mine inspire
>   One virtuous aim, one high resolve impart—
> Light in one drooping soul a hallowed fire,
>   Or bind one broken heart;
>
> Death would be sweeter then,
>   More calm my slumber 'neath the silent sod,
> Might I thus live to bless my fellow-men,
>   Or glorify my God.

O Thou, whose touch can lend
Life to the dead, Thy quickening grace supply;
And grant me, swanlike, my last breath to spend
In song that may not die.

Truly this prayer was answered, for on the afternoon of the day upon which he preached his last sermon he took a walk beside his beloved sea, whose changing moods he had so often witnessed. He then spent some time in the privacy of his own room, from which he came forth with a written copy of "Abide With Me."

On the next day he started on his journey toward Italy, but when he reached Nice, France, it was evident that he could go no farther, and here he died on the twentieth of November, 1847. His last words were "Peace! Joy!" He was buried in the English cemetery of the French city.

A Philadelphia clergyman, the Reverend George D. Baker, while on a trip to Europe, visited the poet's grave at Nice. He found beside it a young man with tear-stained face, who related how, through Mr. Lyte's great hymn, he had been led to Christ.

Mr. Lyte wrote the music for the hymn, but in 1861 Dr. William Henry Monk, of London, England, composed, "in ten minutes," the appealing tune to which it since has been sung.

The great popularity of this hymn was demonstrated by the result of a survey made by an English magazine in 1887. This magazine asked its readers to send in lists of what they considered the best one hundred hymns. About thirty-five hundred sent in lists, and "Abide With Me" received second place. "Rock of Ages," Augustus M. Toplady's great hymn, was the only one receiving a larger number of votes. No doubt a similar survey today would reveal that Mr. Lyte's hymn has lost none of its appeal to human hearts.

The singing of this hymn has often awakened hallowed memories and caused wandering feet to come back to the paths of righteousness. Silas H. Paine, in *Stories of the Great Hymns of the Church*, tells of a young man who left his country home and took up his residence in New York. He was soon swept away by the temptations of the great metropolis, and gave himself up to a life of sin. One day he was making his way along the street to keep an engagement with vicious companions, when there came floating to him on the evening air the sound of singing. He listened, and the words which he heard were those of the hymn, "Abide With Me." A storehouse of memory, long locked, was suddenly opened. The image of his mother came before him, as she sat beside his bed in childhood—a nightly custom—and sang this song. There upon the sidewalk, he was arrested in his downward course. He made his way to the church where the song was being sung, and surrendered his life to Jesus Christ.

John Callahan heard "Abide With Me," sung in a mission. He had not heard it since childhood, when at the age of six he heard it sung at his mother's funeral. The song brought him to his senses and to the realization that he was on the downward road, and he faced about, gave his heart to God, and became a Christian worker. For years he was superintendent of the Hadley Mission in New York City.

A little girl, lying upon a bed of sickness one night heard the ringing of the chimes, and asked what was the music.   Her mother replied that the name of the hymn was "Abide With Me," and that the words of the part just played were,

> Help of the helpless,
> O abide with me!

The little girl expressed her pleasure at the hymn, and manifested the inspiration it had given her in her efforts toward recovery. This hymn has brought faith and courage and triumph to many another invalid fighting against some depressing malady.

It had a strong appeal to the English soldiers in their encampments in the first World War, and it is said that "In life, in death, O Lord, abide with me," had a special and personal significance under the circumstances.

A company of soldiers, also in the first World War, marching in the impenetrable gloom of a starless night in order to take their places to "go over the top" in the early morning, were heard singing,

> Abide with me; fast falls the eventide;
> The darkness deepens; Lord, with me abide.

Some years ago, a company of miners were entrapped in a mine at Cherry, Illinois. A number of them perished but the *Christian Herald* tells of a group that were rescued after a few days, who, through their entombment, had been heartened by the courage and faith of one of their companions, Bill Cleland. As the rescuers neared their friends, they heard the voice of Bill Cleland singing softly "Abide With Me."

This hymn is said to have been the favorite of General Charles George Gordon, the hero of the

Soudan, better known as "Chinese Gordon," for his military achievements in China.

It was the last hymn sung by Miss Edith Cavell before she was executed by the Germans in Belgium on October 12, 1915, because of her efforts in behalf of the English prisoners of war.

It was played at the funeral of former President William Howard Taft.

In *Famous Hymns of the World,* Allan Sutherland relates the following incident, which he quotes from Chaplain C. Q. Wright: "At the Naval Hospital at Norfolk, during the war with Spain, when I conducted the funeral of a poor lad who died there, his shipmates stood around the coffin and joined tearfully in the hymn, 'Abide With Me.'"

Many a saint of God, setting out upon the journey to the land beyond, has been greatly comforted by the words of this hymn.

Dr. Theodore L. Cuyler, who was for thirty years pastor of the Lafayette Avenue Presbyterian Church in Brooklyn, New York, was a great pastor as well as preacher. On January 12, 1902, he preached a sermon in his old church upon the occasion of his eightieth birthday.

His text was from the seventh verse of the fourteenth chapter of Zechariah: "At evening time it shall be light." He related this incident: "I recall an hour spent years ago in a room where one of God's faithful handmaidens was closing life with a most excruciating malady. The end was coming near. I stood to hear a far-off token word from the eternities and catch a far gleam from the throne.

I shall never forget the pathos of her utterance when she repeated:

> Abide with me fast falls the eventide;
>
> .   .   .   .
>
> Hold Thou Thy cross before my closing eyes;
> Shine thro' the gloom, and point me to the skies,
> Heav'n's morning breaks, and earth's vain shadows flee—
> In life, in death, O Lord, abide with me."[1]

Whether the valley through which we pass is only an incident in life's journey, or ends on the land eternal, this hymn is of great comfort as we travel through its shadows.

[1]From *The Homiletic Review*, copyrighted, 1902, by Funk and Wagnalls Company, and used by permission.

II

ALL HAIL THE POWER OF
JESUS' NAME

The missionary's boat was being piloted up the broad waters of an African river. The scenery was wild and picturesque. There were towering forests, matted jungles, and seemingly interminable marshes. It was in 1908, and the missionary, Dr. George Grenfell, was voyaging on the Lomami, one of the great tributaries of the Congo River.

Twenty years before this he had traveled this same stream. At that time the natives had never seen a steamer, and many had never beheld a white man. They looked upon him and all strangers as intruders, and their enmity was manifest. The roll of the war drums was heard through the forests. Time and again the missionary party saw the savage warriors naked on the riverbank, at some point of vantage, bearing their spears, and bows and arrows, and hideous in their war paint. Several times they were attacked, and subjected to flights of arrows.

Now, after the lapse of years, Dr. Grenfell again is passing through this one-time hostile territory, and yonder in the distance the natives are gathered once more on the bank of the river. He hears the sound of voices, but not the bloodcurdling war cry, as of old, but their voices are lifted in the praises of Jehovah, and they are singing among other hymns, "All Hail the Power of Jesus' Name."

The *Life of George Grenfell*, by George Hawker, contains a letter from Dr. Grenfell describing this incident. He says: "The singing, as singing, was often very poor, but there was no doubting the heartiness with which they sang. Even before the engines stopped, and while we were some distance off, the strains reached us. Remembering what I could remember about these places, one is not inclined to criticize the singing. For myself my heart was too full, and I had to join in.

"Some of these places I had seen in the possession of the Arab raiders, some of them I had seen still smoking, after the raiders had done their worst and burned them out. In all of them wickedness and cruelty had had a long, long reign, and the people had suffered many sorrows. But now, surely was the beginning of better days, for was not this the beginning of the rising of the 'Sun of righteousness, with healing in His wings'? God has indeed been good to me, to let me see the dawn of such a day."

In the number gathered to welcome the missionary were those in whose breasts once beat the untamed heart of the savage, but who, now, crowned the Saviour "Lord of all."

The hymn, "All Hail the Power of Jesus' Name," was written by the Reverend Edward Perronet in the year 1779, and was published in 1780, in *The Gospel Magazine*. Perronet was born in 1726, and was the son of the Reverend Vincent Perronet, vicar of Shoreham, in Kent, England.

He shared the religious zeal of the Wesleys, and became closely associated with them in religious work. He attracted the attention of Lady Huntingdon, and was one of the preachers appointed under her patronage. However, he wrote an article attacking the union of church and state, which offended her, and he lost his position.

He also advocated the withdrawal of the followers of John Wesley from the Anglican Church, and the formation of a separate organization. This Wesley opposed, and there came somewhat of an estrangement between them. But afterward this course was pursued, and the great Methodist Episcopal Church was established.

Perronet became the pastor of a dissenting congregation in Canterbury, where he died on January 22, 1792. He was a man of religious fervor and deep piety.

His last words were:

> Glory to God in the height of His divinity,
> Glory to God in the depth of His humanity,
> Glory to God in His all sufficiency,
> And into His hands I commend my spirit.

The tune to which this hymn first was sung in England was composed by William Shrubsole, an intimate friend of Perronet's. It first was called "Miles' Lane," after the name of the chapel, of which Mr. Shrubsole was organist for many years.

But the tune, "Coronation," which is used in America, was composed by Oliver Holden, who was born in Shirley, Massachusetts, in 1765.

Simply to hear this hymn sung only once is sufficient to enable one to understand its universal popularity, and to appreciate its appropriateness for any religious service.

Dr. A. B. Earle, in his volume of reminiscences, *Bringing in Sheaves*, tells of the organization of a church in Albany, New York. He says: "This was done on Thursday. The following Sabbath, I baptized forty-four happy converts, and administered the Lord's Supper in the evening. On that occasion

'All Hail the Power of Jesus' Name' was sung as I had never heard it sung before."

The sentiment of this hymn must be the feeling of the followers of Jesus, whether they are launching a new church enterprise, or worshiping in a congregation of lengthened years.

In *The Missionary Review of the World*, the story is told how one church changed its plan of Christmas celebration. A few weeks before Christmas, a teacher in the Primary department asked the children, "Who was born on Christmas Day?" and they eagerly answered, "Santa Claus." This answer distressed the teacher. She realized that there had been a serious defect in the teaching of both the home and the Sunday school, and she pondered the matter earnestly and prayerfully.

She found the pastor, the superintendent of the school, and other workers in full accord with her desire to exalt Jesus Christ in the Christmas exercises. And so what is called a "White Christmas" was arranged. It was announced that the pupils, instead of receiving gifts, would themselves be givers. They entered enthusiastically into the plan. The object of Christmas was emphasized, it was shown to be the celebration of God's greatest gift to the world, his own Son to be our Redeemer.

Many gifts were brought that evening—gifts for mission hospitals, gifts for the needy in the home city, and gifts to meet other needs at home and abroad. At the close of the service, the congregation sang "All Hail the Power of Jesus' Name." No more appropriate composition could be sung at the Christmas time than Perronet's worshipful hymn.

On the next Sunday when the Primary teacher asked her class who was born on Christmas, they all replied, "The little Lord Jesus."

About forty years ago, Mr. and Mrs. William Raws had a vision of a religious center in the pines of New Jersey. They had no money, but the American Keswick is an answer to their faith. "All Hail the Power of Jesus' Name" was the first hymn sung at its opening.

This hymn was used repeatedly in the sessions of the Baptist World Alliance in Philadelphia in 1911, and appropriately so, for there were gathered there men and women from the homeland, and from distant climes. A number had suffered great hardships for the gospel's sake. They had been stoned and imprisoned, and otherwise persecuted. Some were expecting that as soon as they should return to their native land they would be compelled to stand trial for preaching the truths of God's Word. However, regardless of persecution in the past, and the prospect of its continuance in the future, with glad hearts they mingled their voices with the servants of the Lord from free lands as they sang "Crown Him Lord of all."

In the World's Sunday School Convention in 1904, the audience sang "All Hail the Power of Jesus' Name," and then, very fittingly, representatives from various nations of the earth, far separated from one another, gave their testimony why every tribe should "Crown Him Lord of all."

In the year 1900, there was held in New York City The Ecumenical Conference on Foreign Missions. It was one of the greatest missionary gatherings ever convened in this or in any other land.

Shortly after this meeting, Dr. Louis Albert Banks wrote of it in *The Homiletic Review:* "Edward Perronet's Glorious hymn, 'All Hail the Power of Jesus' Name,' has been sung on many splendid occasions, but taken all together it was never used on an occasion that represented so much of glory and honor to Jesus as when it was sung as the keynote at the opening of the great Ecumenical Conference on Foreign Missions in New York. The whole audience which packed the Carnegie Hall to the last limit of its capacity, led by George C. Stebbins, sang the triumphal hymn with a fervor and an ardor never surpassed by so great an audience on earth."[1]

Dr. Newman Hall was in Athens, Greece, on a Good Friday, years ago, and in the afternoon he preached on Mars Hill. It was here that the apostle Paul, in the first century, seeing the city wholly given to idolatry, courageously preached Christ and him risen from the dead. About fifty Greeks and Americans gathered to hear Dr. Hall on this historic spot, and they sang this coronation hymn.

There are two incidents related by Dr. Duffield in his *English Hymns,* published in 1886 by Funk and Wagnalls, New York, which are often told, but they are well worth repeating. He tells the story of Rev. E. P. Scott, a missionary to India, who heard of a bloodthirsty tribe in the mountains, to whom no one had taken the gospel message, and he decided to go to them. His friends endeavored to dissuade him on account of the great risk to his life, but he replied that he "must carry Jesus to them."

As he was proceeding along a wild mountain path, he was suddenly confronted by a band of armed warriors, who pointed their spears ready to

---

[1]Copyrighted by Funk and Wagnalls Company, and used by permission.

plunge them into his body. Taking out his violin which he always carried, he offered a silent prayer, closed his eyes, and began to play Perronet's great hymn. When he looked again, he found that the spears had been lowered and the natives were manifesting a friendly attitude toward him. He accompanied them to their home, and thus began a work of grace among these savage people.

The other incident is that of the Reverend William Dawson. Dr. Duffield says " 'Billy Dawson,' as he was familiarly styled, was a man of genius, and in his sermon on the offices of Christ he showed it. He had portrayed the Saviour as teacher and priest, and he proceeded to set forth his glory as a king in his own right over saints and angels. Kindling at the thought, he drew the picture of a coronation pageant. The great procession was arrayed. Prophets and patriarchs, apostles and martyrs moved grandly on. The vast temple was filled, and at the climax of the thought, the preacher suddenly broke from his ordinary tone, and sang with startling effect, 'All Hail the Power of Jesus' Name.' 'The effect,' says Christophers, 'was overwhelming. The crowd sprang to their feet, and sang the hymn with a feeling and a power which seemed to swell higher and higher at every verse.' Such was the grand result of Edward Perronet's verses."[2]

No hymn is truly great that does not lead men and women into closer relationship to God, and bring comfort to human souls.

The story is related of a Christian woman who was stricken mortally ill at the Paris Exposition. In her weakness she managed to say, "Bring." Her friends brought her food and various delicacies, all

[2]Copyrighted by Funk and Wagnalls Company, and used by permission.

of which she refused, but she repeated the word "Bring." Finally, summoning all her strength, she exclaimed: "Bring forth the royal diadem, and crown Him Lord of all." And she passed on to receive her own crown of life.

George T. B. Davis, in *Twice Around the World with Alexander*, tells the story of a godless young man who, while standing upon a London street, waiting to get into a theater, heard the singing of "All Hail the Power of Jesus' Name." He perceived that it was coming from the tabernacle across the street, where the Torrey-Alexander meetings were being held. The song awakened sacred memories of a righteous home. Turning his back upon the theater, he crossed the street and went into the tabernacle. There he consecrated his life to God.

Potentate, as well as peasant, needs to exalt Jesus Christ. It is related that upon one occasion, Queen Victoria said that she wished the Lord would come during her lifetime. Being asked by one of her chaplains why she entertained this desire, she replied: "I should so love to lay my crown at his feet." The Lord did not need her crown, but he wanted her heart, and the noble queen had already given that to him.

Dr. James Sibree, in the closing sentences of his book, *Fifty Years in Madagascar*, expresses the hope that his narrative of the work of grace accomplished in that island might hasten the time "when Jesus Christ shall be acknowledged everywhere as 'Lord of all.'"

But let us remember that if we are to crown "Him Lord of all," we first must crown him, Lord of the individual heart and life.

III

ALMOST PERSUADED

A gawky barefoot boy was walking down the street of a Pennsylvania village. Suddenly he heard the sweetest music to which he had ever listened. He perceived that it was coming from the open door of a near-by residence; and toward it he seemed almost irresistibly drawn. Almost unconscious of what he was doing, he entered the home unobserved, and stood in the door of the parlor, listening to a young lady playing upon a piano, the first that he had ever seen. He was so entranced by the melody, that when she ceased playing, he impulsively exclaimed: "O lady, play some more." Somewhat startled by the sound of a voice, she wheeled, and saw the awkward boy standing before her, and harshly exclaimed: "Go out of here with your great feet."

The boy turned away crestfallen and went out into the street. Upon this occasion, this young woman lost, no doubt, the greatest opportunity that ever came to her, and one which any individual might well covet. If she had manifested sympathy for the lad, spoken kindly to him, and helped him gratify his hunger for music, she might have rendered a signal service, not only for him, but for the world, and her name would have become associated with one of the sweetest singers of the land, for the boy's name was Philip Bliss, known afterward to fame as the wonderful singer, P. P. Bliss.

Philip Bliss was born in Clearfield County, Pennsylvania, on July 9, 1838. The boy had few advan-

tages in his early years. The family was in moderate
circumstances, and school facilities were quite mea-
ger. At the age of eleven, he left home to support
himself by working on a farm. When he was thirteen he was a farm hand at thirteen dollars a month.
In the next few years, we find him cutting logs,
working in a lumber camp, and busy at a sawmill.
Whenever he could do so, he went to school. In
1850, he attended a revival meeting, was converted,
and joined a Baptist church.

When he was eighteen years old he worked on a
farm in the summer and taught school in the winter.
In 1858 he was appointed a teacher in the Rome
Academy at Rome, Pennsylvania. Here he met and
married Miss Lucy Young. She was of a musical
family and greatly encouraged him in developing
his musical talents. The young woman was an earnest member of a Presbyterian church, and he joined
her in its membership.

It was the day of the old-fashioned singing school,
which was frequently conducted by a teacher traveling from place to place. Young Bliss delighted
to attend these exercises, and his musical ability
began to attract the attention of his friends. He
soon became a teacher of one of these schools, but
he recognized and greatly deplored his limitations.
His great desire was to study under some accomplished musician.

When a Normal Academy of music was held in a
neighboring town, he was especially interested and
diligently studied its program. He longed to avail
himself of its splendid advantages, but was not
financially able to do so. So keen was his disappointment that he threw himself upon the settee
in the living room, and speaking of the occasion,

he says: "I just cried for disappointment. I thought everything had come to an end; that my life must be passed as a farm hand and country schoolmaster, and all bright hopes for the future must be given up."

But Mrs. Allen, his wife's grandmother, saw his distress, and upon being told the cause of it, her sympathetic heart was touched. When she learned that it would take thirty dollars to finance the enterprise, she said: "Well, thirty dollars is a good deal of money. I have an old stocking that I have been dropping pieces of silver in for a good many years, and I'll just see how much there is. Perhaps there are thirty dollars, and if there are, why, you can take it and go to the Normal."

The stocking yielded up the thirty dollars, and Philip Bliss attended the school, and then in 1860, he took up the occupation of professional music teacher. He says in his diary, "Old Fanny (a horse) and a twenty-dollar melodeon furnished by O. F. Young set me up in the profession." He still, however, pursued his studies and the training of his voice.

His first song, "Lora Vale," was published in 1865. It was a song of tender sentiment, but without special religious emphasis. It was not long, however, before he consecrated his pen to productions of deep spiritual significance.

Mr. Bliss accepted a position with a music house in Chicago, and was employed in the holding of musical conventions and the giving of sacred concerts. In 1869, he met Mr. D. L. Moody, who urged him to give up his business and become a singing evangelist. This he did some years later. Major D. W. Whittle relates the circumstances of this decision.

He and Mr. Bliss were holding a meeting together in Waukegan, Illinois. At first little interest was manifested, but one evening Mr. Bliss sang "Almost Persuaded," and the power of God filled the house, and there were a number of conversions. The following services were full of spiritual power. It was at this meeting that both Major Whittle and Mr. Bliss decided to give up business engagements and devote their entire time to evangelism.

Mr. Bliss wrote many hymns of great popularity. Among them are "Jesus Loves Even Me," "Hold the Fort," and "Let the Lower Lights Be Burning." But perhaps the hymn of his which has been most used, and is most familiar to the public, is "Almost Persuaded."

Upon one occasion when Mr. Bliss was listening to a sermon by his friend, the Reverend Mr. Brundage, the minister closed his appeal with these words: "He who is almost persuaded is almost saved. But to be almost saved is to be eternally lost." These words impressed the singer and led him to write this great hymn, which has been the means of leading many souls to Jesus.

George C. Stebbins, himself a singer of note, speaks of the beauty and impressiveness of this hymn, and calls it a "classic in its way."

Ira D. Sankey said he felt that "Almost Persuaded" had won more souls to Christ than any other hymn Mr. Bliss had written. Mr. Sankey often sang this hymn with wonderful effect. It was used a great deal in the Moody and Sankey meetings. In one of the services in New York, those who wished to talk on religious matters were requested to go into the inquiry room. "Almost Persuaded" and "Just As I Am" were sung, and about two hundred responded to the invitation.

In a meeting in Liverpool, England, Mr. Sankey sang "Almost Persuaded," and Mr. Moody said that there were so many who were anxious about their souls, he would not be able to speak to them individually, and he counseled them to go home, take God's Word, plead the promises of the Lord and commit themselves to him. And he prayed that they might not be simply almost, but altogether persuaded.

At the close of one of the meetings in London, Mr. Sankey sang this great hymn, and those who were concerned about religion were invited to remain after the benediction, and several thousand kept their seats. Mr. Sankey, in his *Story of the Gospel Hymns*, says that one of the most impressive occasions upon which this hymn was sung was when he sang it in London before an audience of fifteen thousand people, among whom was the great statesman, William E. Gladstone.

When this hymn was sung by Mr. Sankey in Philadelphia, many were awakened by it, among which number was an attorney. He came forward and said that he was not only "almost" but "altogether persuaded" to trust Jesus as his Saviour.

Some years ago, two sisters were alone in their London home, their widowed mother, a Mrs. Lee, having gone out on an errand. Lucy, the older, was a Christian, and now welcomed this opportunity of endeavoring to lead her younger sister to Christ. She began to play several hymns. Finally while she was singing "Almost Persuaded," the younger girl became greatly moved, and that evening yielded her youthful heart to Jesus. Minnie L. Carpenter relates in *The Angel Adjutant*, a biography of Miss Kate Lee, how this young girl consecrated her life to the service of the Redeemer, and how, through her work in the Salvation Army, she led many a broken life to the healing touch of her Lord.

Major D. W. Whittle, the biographer of Mr. Bliss, received many letters from ministers telling of how the singing of "Almost Persuaded" had produced great results in their meetings.

In *The Wonderful Career of Moody and Sankey,* by Dr. E. J. Goodspeed, is given this account of a watch-night service held in Philadelphia by Mr. Moody on the last night of 1875, in which the evangelist had been urging the unsaved to accept Jesus Christ as their Saviour before the closing of the old year.

Dr. Goodspeed says: "At fifteen minutes to twelve, Mr. Moody asked that all join in a silent prayer. Heads were bowed all over the building, and silence reigned, Mr. Sankey breaking it by playing the soft strains of 'Almost Persuaded,' which he sang, or rather recited, in a broken voice. Mr. Moody asked those Christians to rise who wished other Christians to pray for them. Almost the entire audience rose to their feet. Then the unconverted were requested to stand up and ask the Christians for their prayers. Rev. Mr. Johns led in prayer, remembering both classes—the converted in need of help, and the unconverted in need of a Saviour."

Silas H. Paine, in *Stories of Great Hymns of the Church,* relates this incident, which was told by a writer in *Christian Secretary.* "In a mission of this great city (New York) a few evenings ago, there sat among the motley and changing audience a young man whose face had a kindly look. All unnoticed he sat, until in a pause he rose, saying, 'Please sing seventy-five,' and took his seat. The first stanza of 'Almost Persuaded' was sung when the leader said, 'I want to ask that young man if he is a Christian.'

"Calmly rising, a young man of perhaps twenty years, fairly clothed, not a vicious but an undecided face, replied: 'No, I am not a Christian, but I learned that piece in the Sunday school. I was brought up in a quiet little country village in the southern part of the United States. There I went to church and Sunday school, where I learned this hymn. I always went to church until I came to New York, then I began to run around, but I never hear that piece sung but I am almost persuaded to become a Christian.' I wish that I might record that he did then and there give his heart to Christ; but like too many others we fear he put it off to a more convenient season."

The refrain in each heart should be not "almost!" "almost!" but "fully!" "fully!" persuaded "now to believe."

In December, 1876, Mr. and Mrs. Bliss visited their old home in Rome, Pennsylvania. On their return, the heavily loaded passenger train, upon which they were riding, was nearing the station at Ashtabula, Ohio, when it plunged through a trestle seventy-five feet high. The wreckage caught fire, and one hundred people perished in this catastrophe. No trace of the bodies of the singer and his wife was ever discovered.

Perhaps the passing of no other private citizen had brought such grief to the land. Memorial services were held throughout the country, at which the hymns of Mr. Bliss, prominent among them "Almost Persuaded," were sung by sorrowing multitudes.

IV

BLEST BE THE TIE THAT BINDS

The unpretentious Baptist parsonage at Wainsgate, England, was the scene of unusual activity. Wagons were drawn up in front of it, and men were busy carrying out of the house various articles of furniture, chairs, beds, cases, and books—books, for the minister was a studious man. Four or five wagons had already been loaded, and now the last one was at the door, and in a few moments the small cavalcade was to start for the great city of London.

The members of the little church were devoted to their pastor and his noble wife, because of their faithful labors among them, and they gathered around with tear-stained faces.

The minister and his wife, sharing the grief of their friends, sat upon one of the packing cases and joined in the weeping. Finally the wife exclaimed: "O John! John! I cannot bear this. I do not know how to go." "Nor I either," replied her husband, "nor will we go." Then came the order to unload the wagons and put everything back in the place where it was before.

And thus the decision was made, and the Reverend and Mrs. John Fawcett decided to remain with the small and poor congregation at Wainsgate, instead of going to London to take charge of a prominent church in that metropolitan city to which the minister had been called.

It is said that in this experience came the inspiration for Dr. Fawcett's great hymn, "Blest Be the Tie That Binds."

John Fawcett was born on January 6, 1739, at Lidget Green, near Bradford, Yorkshire, England. Young Fawcett knew the privations of childhood, for when he was eleven years old his father died, leaving the widowed mother in humble circumstances, and with several children to support. When the boy was eleven years old, he was apprenticed, according to English custom, to a trader in Bradford with whom he remained for six years.

When he was sixteen years old, he was converted under the preaching of George Whitefield, who used as his text upon that occasion, "And as Moses lifted up the serpent in the wilderness, even so must the Son of man be lifted up." Writing of this event afterward, he said: "As long as life remains, I shall remember both the text and the sermon."

In 1758, young Fawcett united with the recently organized Baptist church at Bradford, and from the very first he became active in the work of the organization.

His heart soon turned toward the gospel ministry, and he gave serious thought to the question of entering this noble calling. He realized, however, that the decision was not a light one to make and he gave it earnest consideration and prayer.

He wrote in his diary: "O Lord, I know not what to do, but my eyes are upon Thee. If in thy wise counsel, thou hast fixed upon me to bear thy name to Gentile sinners, I earnestly implore that thou wouldst give me the right spirit, and bestow upon me every needful qualification for that most difficult and important work. If thou dost not call me to do it, O Father, not my will, but thine be done."

Finally, he made his choice and began to preach. In February, 1764, he took charge of the little Baptist church at Wainsgate, in Yorkshire, and on July

31 of the following year he was ordained to the ministry. The church was small and the community poor, but the young pastor gave himself with consecrated zeal to the needs of the congregation.

He was a young man of noble attainments, and it is not surprising that he received a call to become pastor of a London church. It was the church which Dr. John Gill served for many years. He naturally desired a wider sphere of influence and increased revenue to meet the needs of his growing family. But when the time came for his departure to the city, he could not tear himself away from his beloved Wainsgate, and here he abode as pastor until nearly the close of his useful life.

Several books came from the pen of Dr. Fawcett, and a number of hymns were written by him. Among the most notable of his hymns are

> Blest be the tie that binds
> Our hearts in Christian love.

and

> Lord, dismiss us with thy blessing
> Fill our hearts with joy and peace.

An interesting incident is related concerning a small volume which Dr. Fawcett wrote on "Anger." A copy came into the hands of the king, George III. The monarch was greatly pleased with it, and offered to confer on Dr. Fawcett any favor which he might desire. The offer was greatly appreciated by the minister, who, nevertheless, felt that he could not accept it.

However, sometime afterward the son of one of his intimate friends committed forgery, and was sentenced to be hanged, that being the penalty at the time for that crime. Dr. Fawcett interceded with the king on behalf of the young man, and the monarch, remembering his promise, granted a pardon.

The hymn, "Blest Be the Tie That Binds," is suitable to be sung in every gathering of Christian worshipers regardless of any diversity of race, creed, color or age, for the hearts of God's people are bound together by the cords of Christian love the whole world around.

During the Torrey-Alexander meetings in Albert Hall, London, England, many attended, not only from the different sections of the city, but various nationalities were represented. One night, while the audience was singing "Blest Be the Tie That Binds," the question was asked how many different nationalities had members in the audience. It was ascertained that, including England, there were fifteen. Men and women were present from the following countries: America, Switzerland, France, Germany, Russia, Japan, Sweden, Norway, Denmark, Scotland, Ireland, Wales, Holland, and Australia. With zestful enthusiasm, they mingled their voices in singing this great fellowship hymn.

When the delegates from America were on their way to the World's Sunday School Convention in Rome in 1907, an inspiring religious service was conducted on board the steamship *Neckar*, which was conveying one hundred fifty-four of the five hundred American delegates to the convention. In the Sunday school exercises of the occasion, a birthday recognition service was held and "Blest Be the Tie" was sung. As those words floated out upon the waters of the deep, they were emblematical of the union of Christian hearts, whether God's people sailed the seas, or dwelt far from the sounding waves.

At the Sunday School Convention held in Jerusalem in 1904, His Excellency, Joseph Pasha, former
mayor of the city, made a brief address which he
closed by reading impressively the nineteenth
Psalm, and the audience joined in singing "Blest Be
the Tie That Binds." And surely the Christian love
that binds together the diverse elements of human
nature in devout worship, and blends the babel of
human voices into harmonious song does more to
declare the glory of God than even do the mighty
works of nature about us.

This is indeed a popular and appropriate convention song. In the following year, 1905, the Sunday
School Convention met in Toronto, Canada. At this
convention, there was strong division upon certain
questions of policy. When the president announced
that the period for discussion had expired, and the
time had arrived for a vote, he asked that it might
be preceded by a prayer and a hymn, and the hymn
selected was "Blest Be the Tie That Binds." The
words seemed to have a prophetic implication, for
a controversial question was settled quickly, with
good will and unanimity.

When the time came for the final adjournment,
the president, Justice Maclaren, requested Dr. Potts
to dismiss and close the convention. Dr. Potts said:
"My dear friends, it is probable that many who hear
my voice tonight will gather at Louisville. It is
equally probable that voices that have been heard
here will not be heard again at an international
convention. At Jerusalem, we joined hands and
sang 'Blest Be the Tie That Binds.' Let us do the
same here."

The hymn was sung, the closing prayer offered,
and the convention adjourned to meet the following

year in Louisville, Kentucky, where the hymn was again sung.

At the Zurich Convention of the same organization in 1913, Dr. F. B. Meyer led a consecration service. He asked the members of the great congregation to repeat, each one in his own tongue, "For God so loved the world, that he gave his only begotten Son, that whosoever believeth in him should not perish, but have everlasting life." In various languages these words were spoken, and then the same voices joined in singing "Blest Be the Tie That Binds."

When Dr. Russell H. Conwell presented the Reverend William Fetler from Russia to the Baptist World Alliance, meeting in Philadelphia in 1911, he said: "What welcome can we give to Brother Fetler? What can we do more than to rise and say, 'God bless you' and sing 'Blest be the tie that binds our hearts in Christian love'? Brother Fetler, we welcome you with all our souls."

Mr. Fetler had been indicted in Russia for preaching the gospel, and was under police surveillance in order to prevent him from escaping from the country before his trial. He was anxious to come to Philadelphia to the meeting of the Alliance. The government at first refused permission, but at last consented, when he posted a twenty-five hundred dollar cash bond, which was furnished by the Alliance, thus demonstrating the truthfulness of the words of this hymn,

> We share our mutual woes,
> Our mutual burdens bear.

In a Southern Methodist church in northern Alabama, the women had been working in two separate missionary societies, one for home missions and one for foreign missions. Finally it was decided to consolidate the two. A unique "wedding ceremony" was celebrated; at the close of which the united society sang "Blest Be the Tie That Binds."

Often when God's people have met together in family groups, this is the hymn sung in separating. Dr. and Mrs. Miles Bronson, who had been missionaries to Assam in India for a number of years (and who, in fact, were the first missionaries to teach Christ to the savage tribes of Assam), were returning to America in 1868, both fully expecting to go back to their labors on the foreign field. During the voyage, Mrs. Bronson was lying upon a sofa in the cabin, when a sudden lurch of the ship threw her violently to the floor, breaking her hip and inflicting other injuries.

Shortly after reaching this country she was taken to Springfield, New York, from where it was decided that she should go to Chicago to spend the winter with a daughter. A little farewell service was held by her friends and relatives, and "Blest Be the Tie," was sung with sad hearts and trembling voices, for the singers felt that the "hope to meet again" would be realized only in the land beyond. It was not long before this devoted missionary bade good-by to earthly scenes.

In a beautiful room in New York City in February, 1898, a small group of weeping women gaththered around the bed of Miss Frances E. Willard, as that heroic soul breathed her last. With tears streaming down their cheeks they gently sang,

> Blest be the tie that binds
> Our hearts in Christian love;
> The fellowship of kindred minds
> Is like to that above.

In the early part of 1816, Dr. Fawcett was stricken with paralysis and had to relinquish his pastoral duties; and on July 25, 1817, this great minister and poet passed away. Among his last words were, "Come, Lord Jesus, come quickly."

V

SAFE IN THE ARMS OF JESUS

The name Fanny Crosby is a household word in many a home of the lovers of inspiring song, but perhaps comparatively few know that, in 1858, she was married to Mr. Alexander Van Alstyne, who was a musician, and blind student in the same institution with Miss Crosby.

When they were married, she suggested the adoption of "Mrs. Van Alstyne," in her writing, but her husband insisted on her continuing to use her maiden name, and this she did, sending it around the world with her songs. For forty years this married life was a happy one; and then, in 1902, Mr. Van Alstyne passed away, being survived by his widow for nearly thirteen years longer.

Fanny Crosby was born on March 24, 1820, in Putnam County, New York. When she was six weeks old the improper treatment of an eye affection permanently destroyed her sight. However she was a happy child, and was possessed of a buoyancy of spirit that smoothed out many rough places for her.

At the age of eight years, she wrote her first poem, which contained her philosophy of life, not only for childhood, but for all the many years of her earthly sojourn. It began,

> O what a happy soul I am;
> Although I cannot see,
> I am resolved that in this world,
> Contented I will be.

As a child she listened avidly to any reading that was done for her, and developed a remarkable memory. When she was ten years old, she could recite the first five books of the Old Testament, and the first four books of the New Testament.

Arthur Dixon, writing in *The Sunday School Times* of an interview with Miss Crosby a few days before she celebrated her ninety-third birthday, says: "She told me that the ready availability of the Bible language proved invaluable to her in her writing and in her life." Speaking of her blindness, she said to him: "I have no affliction. What is the loss of one little faculty, when it has helped me to so many opportunities? My whole life might have lost its usefulness, if I had not been blind."

Throughout life her attitude toward her blindness was one of resignation. She accepted it as providential, and refused to let it interfere with her happiness, her faith, or her usefulness. She walked in physical but not in spiritual darkness, for the light of another world illumined her soul.

She eagerly longed for an education, and when she was fifteen years old, her heart was thrilled at learning that arrangements had been made to send her to the New York School for the Blind. This school had been in operation only a short while, but was said to be the best school of its kind in this country. She manifested such aptitude for learning that in ten years she was made a teacher in the institution.

Upon one occasion, a party was sent from the school to Congress to endeavor to secure an appropriation for its work. Miss Crosby delivered several of her poetical compositions to the lawmakers. It was a notable assembly which she addressed, for in it were such men as John Quincy Adams, James

Buchanan, Andrew Johnson, Hannibal Hamlin, Stephen A. Douglas, Rufus Choate, Thomas H. Benton, Hamilton Fish, Henry A. Wise, Alexander Stevens, Jefferson Davis, and Robert Toombs.

When Henry Clay visited the school Miss Crosby was selected to recite a poem in his honor. When she had finished, Mr. Clay took her by the hand, and turning to the audience, said: "This is not the only poem for which I am indebted to this lady. Six months ago, she sent me some lines on the death of my dear son." And standing there the great statesman and the blind poet wept together. Mr. Clay's son had been killed in the battle of Buena Vista, in Mexico.

Miss Crosby enjoyed a long friendship with President Grover Cleveland, whose brother was head teacher in the school which she attended. Upon the death of their father, Grover Cleveland came to the school as its secretary, and the young man copied many of the poet's hymns in his clear, legible handwriting.

She also numbered other presidents among her warm personal friends, Martin Van Buren, John Tyler, and James K. Polk.

Her first hymn beginning

> We are going, we are going,
> To a home beyond the skies,

was written in 1864, at the suggestion of Mr. W. B. Bradbury, himself a noted composer. Thus began a most remarkable career of hymn writing, for she wrote over eight thousand hymns.

W. H. Doane, who composed the music for a number of her hymns, said to the poet one day: "Fanny, I have a tune I would like to have you write words for. He played it over, and Miss Crosby exclaimed:

"That says 'Safe in the arms of Jesus!'" She went to her room, and in about thirty minutes returned with this hymn which has brought comfort to a multitude of sorrowing hearts and which, no doubt, will send its message of consolation down through the centuries.

The words of this hymn lend themselves readily to memorizing, and the life of any child, or adult either, will be richer for laying up its words in the storehouse of memory. Dr. John Gardner, in an address at Northfield, in 1918, said that when a little boy, three years old, he was taught to sing this hymn.

We are not surprised that it is a favorite with all ages in various countries. And we learn that the soldiers in the army who put their trust in the Lord sing this hymn, realizing that even in the clash of battle the everlasting arms are about those who love their God. An English writer tells how feelingly it was sung by the English soldiers in the first World War.

Dr. George F. Pentecost was going to Dr. Bonar's church in Glasgow, Scotland, one Sunday evening. On his way he passed a company of Christian workers holding a street meeting. They were singing "Safe in the Arms of Jesus"; and the rough, motley crowd about them gave earnest heed to the words.

Ira D. Sankey once visited Basel, Switzerland, for a short period of rest. On the evening of his arrival, he heard beautiful singing and, looking out, he saw about fifty people gathered under his window rendering "Safe in the Arms of Jesus." It is indeed comforting to realize that wherever we are, whether at home, or in some distant land, we can have the Saviour's presence and protection.

Mr. Sankey told of a party of tourists who were traveling in the Alps, who began to sing this hymn. When they had finished the first stanza, they were surprised and delighted to hear the sound of the second verse coming to them from a near-by mountain peak. They could not see the other singers, but, alternately, the two groups sang the hymn, with a feeling of security, although the towering mountains and threatening precipices were all about them.

Allan Sutherland, in *Famous Hymns of the World*, tells of two little girls: "One of them had been singing "Safe in the Arms of Jesus," and the other had interrupted her with the question: "How do you know that you are safe?" "Because," was the response, "I am holding on to Jesus with both hands." "But that does not make you safe," persisted the other. "Suppose Satan should cut off your hands." For a moment a troubled expression came into the trustful little face, but it almost instantly cleared and she joyously exclaimed, 'Oh, I made a mistake. Jesus is holding me with his hands, and Satan can't cut his hands off. I am perfectly safe in his arms.' "

Many a wanderer from the fold of God has heard this hymn, and, realizing that instead of being "Safe in the arms of Jesus," he was a poor lost soul, has sought and found redemption because of the influence of these words.

Some years ago, George Young, of Portlock, Ontario, wrote a letter to *The Sunday School Times*, saying that the singing of this hymn at his sister's funeral was the means of leading him to Christ.

The words of this hymn have often mitigated the grief of sorrowing hearts. Dr. John Hall said that this hymn had brought more consolation to bereaved mothers than any other hymn he had ever known.

But it has also brought comfort to many other troubled souls.

A hackman, when he learned that his passenger was Miss Fanny Crosby, took off his hat and wept. He called a policeman, and said: "This is Miss Fanny Crosby, who wrote 'Safe in the Arms of Jesus,'" and asked him to see her safely to the train. "I sure will," he replied. And then he added sadly, "We sang that hymn at my little girl's funeral last week."

Before his brutal murder by the savages of Uganda, Africa, Bishop James Hannington was subjected to great cruelties by his captors. Speaking of the treatment he received at their hands, he says in his journal, which was recovered after his death: "Twice I nearly broke away from them and grew faint with struggling, and was dragged by the legs over the ground. I said: 'Lord, I put myself in Thy hands, I look to Thee alone.' Then another struggle and I got to my feet, and was thus dashed along. More than once I was brought into contact with banana trees, some trying in their haste to force me one way, others the other, and the exertion and struggling strained me in the most agonizing manner. In spite of it all and feeling that I was being dragged away to be murdered at a distance, I sang, 'Safe in the Arms of Jesus,' and then laughed at the very agony of my situation."

A Scotch woman who thought that Mr. Sankey was the author because he had been singing "Safe in the Arms of Jesus," thanked him for it. When she learned that Miss Fanny Crosby had written it, she said: "When you go back to America, give her my love, and tell her that an old Scotch woman sends her blessings. The last hymn my daughter sang before she died was that one."

Miss Crosby describes a visit to her that was made by a lady from England, who was born in the same town with Miss Frances Ridley Havergal and knew her quite well. Miss Crosby said: "My visitor told me that she did not come to see me for herself alone, but to tell me the story of her dear boy, Will, who went home to God two years ago. 'The evening on which he died,' she said, 'was one of those charming English twilights. Will had felt better all day and the doctor encouraged us.

" 'I was alone in the house when I heard the sound of his cane on the floor. On reaching his bedside he said "Mother dear, don't leave me. Give me my hymn-book. I want to sing, 'Safe in the Arms of Jesus.' " When he reached the line "Hark, 'tis the voice of angels," my dear boy dropped the book, and his face was illumined as he said: "Ma, there is the jasper sea." And then he passed out to be with them and his Lord forevermore.' "[1]

Miss Crosby died at her home in Bridgeport, Connecticut on February 12, 1915, just a few weeks before she would have been ninety-five years old.

The Reverend William A. Sunday ("Billy" Sunday), the great evangelist, dictated a letter to her pastor, in which he sent a message of love to the poet telling her that he expected to visit her soon. Just as he had signed the letter a messenger came hurriedly into the room and announced: "I have bad news for you; your old friend Fanny Crosby is dead."

Mr. Sunday was greatly distressed at the message, and voiced the sentiment of thousands when he said: "Fanny Crosby was an angelic woman."

---

[1]From *Fanny Crosby's Story of Ninety-Four Years*, by S. Trevena Jackson. Copyrighted by Fleming H. Revell Company, publishers, and used by permission.

VI

TAKE MY LIFE, AND LET IT BE

The heart of a young girl was longing for spiritual guidance. She wanted to be a Christian, and she wished that someone would talk to her about her soul. She wondered why the minister, who preached as if his heart were full of love for Christ, did not speak to her personally in the family circle about religion. She was greatly interested in this subject, although to those around her she, no doubt, appeared to be a thoughtless and merry child. He spoke of many things and made himself agreeable and interesting, but the one subject, that of religion, which she most desired to hear about he neglected to discuss.

The girl was Frances Ridley Havergal. Miss Havergal was born December 14, 1836, at Astley, Worcestershire, England, where her father was rector of the church for twenty years. Her two brothers were also clergymen, and her three sisters were women of culture and spirituality. When three years old she had learned to read easy books, and one of her sisters says that at the age of four she could read the Bible and any ordinary book, and had learned to write.

The family of Miss Havergal was a literary one, and she grew up in an atmosphere of spiritual and literary culture. Her father received several notable awards for musical compositions. Dr. Samuel W. Duffield says of him in *English Hymns*: "He was one of the best musical composers of his day."

Mr. Havergal was appointed to the Rectory of St. Nicholas in Worcester, and the family moved there in 1845.

Miss Havergal was never strong and robust, and at times her schooling was interfered with on account of ill health. When fifteen years old, it was necessary for her to give up her studies for a while, being almost blind for weeks on account of an attack of erysipelas in her face and head. But she bore her affliction patiently.

She accompanied her father to Germany, where he went to consult a celebrated oculist concerning a serious eye trouble. While in that country, she resumed her studies, and was the only Christian pupil in a school of one hundred ten pupils. Because of her religion, she was the object of many petty annoyances, and even persecution. But the loyalty of this fifteen-year-old girl to the principles of her faith brought honor to her Lord and Master, in that skeptical society.

While she was wonderfully endowed as writer and poet, she refused to allow her natural gifts to become an excuse for the neglect of her studies. She did not confine herself to English composition, but she studied the modern languages, and also became sufficiently proficient in Greek to read the New Testament in that tongue. She obtained a limited knowledge of Hebrew.

She was always ready to sing for the glory of her Lord, and delighted in teaching young girls to play and sing. She was a diligent student of the Bible, and learned by heart the Gospels, the Epistles, Revelation, the Psalms, Isaiah, and the Minor Prophets. She was also possessed of a marvelous musical memory, and could play through Handel and much of Beethoven and Mendelssohn without notes. She particularly delighted in Handel.

In writing the consecration hymn, Miss Havergal was no doubt greatly influenced by a little book which a friend had sent her, *All for Jesus*. She read it and reread it, and it made a profound impression upon her. She wrote to the author: "I do long for deeper and fuller teaching in my own heart. *All for Jesus* has touched me very much."

In December, 1873, shortly after receiving the little book, she composed her great hymn, and she gives the immediate circumstances of its writing in a letter to a friend: "Perhaps you will be interested to know the origin of the consecration hymn, 'Take My Life.' I went for a little visit of five days. There were ten persons in the house, some unconverted and long prayed for, some converted but not rejoicing Christians. He gave me the prayer, 'Lord, give me all in this house.' And He just did! Before I left the house every one had got a blessing. The last night of my visit I was too happy to sleep, and passed most of the night in praise and renewal of my own consecration, and these little couplets formed themsleves and chimed in my heart one after another, till they finished with 'Ever, only, all for Thee.'"

Miss Havergal's little volume, *Kept for the Master's Use*, is a homily on this hymn, and she takes it verse by verse and comments upon it.

In her younger days she wanted to go as a missionary to some heathen land, but her health prevented her from carrying out this cherished hope. She, however, delighted in the organization and encouragement of missionary societies. She gave of her means for the furtherance of this cause, and

finally decided to give her jewelry for this great
work as she thought of her couplet,

> Take my silver and my gold,
> Not a mite would I withhold.

She possessed some valuable pieces, and, after
taking out a few of them for sentimental reasons,
she sent the rest to the missionary society. She remarked: "I had no idea that I had such a jeweler's
shop. Nearly fifty articles are being packed off. I
don't think I need tell you I never packed a box with
such pleasure." She explained in regard to this
sentiment in her hymn that she did not mean that
all our money should be placed in the collection
plate, but that all our possessions, nevertheless,
should be consecrated to the Lord and held at his
disposal.

It is no wonder that this hymn, coming from
one so devoted to her Saviour, has been a blessing
to multitudes, leading them into lives of deeper
consecration.

George T. B. Davis, in *Twice Around the World
With Alexander,* tells of an experience of Mr. Harkness, the pianist, in London. As he was locking his
piano at the close of an afternoon service, a gentleman approached and told him that he was an organist in a London church, and teacher of a Sunday
school class, but that he was not living the right
life. Mr. Harkness talked with him earnestly and
urged him to give up his evil practices, and make a
full surrender to Jesus. The man was greatly
moved but left without expressing any definite decision. However, a few days later, Mr. Harkness
received a letter from him in which he said: "I have

this day surrendered all to Jesus, and asked the
Lord to

Take my hands, and let them move
At the impulse of Thy love.

I have dedicated my piano to the praise of Jesus."

Miss A. O. Stott, who spent a number of years as
a missionary in China, relates in *The Sunday School
Times* the touching story of a Chinese girl, Lee-Lee,
who came to the home of a Mrs. Wong as a child
bride. Her lot was a sad one, for her mother-in-law
was exceedingly cruel, not brooking the slightest
disobedience to her commands.

The young girl had become a Christian before
her marriage, and when Mrs. Wong found her reading the Bible, she forbade her doing so. But the
girl was loyal to her Lord, and kept the Bible hid-
den, as her mother-in-law had threatened to burn
it. She read it whenever opportunity was presented. Mrs. Wong, learning this, became so
incensed that she determined to punish the girl se-
verely, even if it took her life. She ordered that
the feet of the girl which had never been bound
before, should be bound as tightly as possible. She
had her tied up in the stable, and left her alone in
her agony. Here she would have perished misera-
bly, but an older member of the family, returning
home from a journey, was told by neighbors what
had occurred, and he went and cut down the poor
limp, unconscious body.

She was taken to the mission hospital where it
was found necessary to amputate both of her feet.
The cruel mother-in-law refused to take the crippled
girl back into her home, but the missionaries provided her with artificial feet, and gave her a home.

She became a diligent and helpful nurse in the
hospital. She was known as "the Heavenly Foot

One." Her favorite hymn was the one by Miss
Havergal, and often in the discharge of her duties
through the use of her artificial feet, she sang cheer-
fully

> Take my feet, and let them be
> Swift and beautiful for Thee.

A story concerning the use of this hymn in a
Christmas service some years ago in Japan is given,
also in *The Sunday School Times,* by Opal Leonore
Gibbs: "An unexpected bountiful box from a missionary society back home contained popcorn. This
was popped and strung by Betty and Jean, the missionary's small daughters. Kumquats made a lovely
trimming also, a golden one. And rice paste dyed
red was extremely effective as an ornamentation.
Thus the little tree was sweetly and naturally
arrayed.

"The Fujinkai meeting came first, and the house
filled slowly with drab married ladies from various
walks in life. On this particular day the talk was
about 'Sacrifice.' There was praying, too,—always
they did much praying, but before it began, the
Sambika songbooks were opened and everyone sang
very softly,

> Take my life, and let it be
> Consecrated Lord to Thee.

"New faces were present, three or four of them,
faces lacking that inner joy so plainly written on
the others. The leader asked quietly if such would
not now, today, take words, even if ever so few, and
draw near to the living and true God.

"There was a moment of breathing silence, then
a timid voice, a bit broken with tears, responded.
Then another, yes, and a third. And joy filled brim-
ful the hearts of the little circle, for were they not
both giving to Him, whose birthday it was, and re-

ceiving from Him new members in sisterhood fellowship?"[1]

In *The Missionary Review of the World,* Mrs. E. C. Cronk related the following incident: The leader of a missionary society announced Miss Havergal's hymn, and suggested the omission of the third stanza. "Madam President," said a voice from the group, "I am opposed to omitting that third stanza."

Says Mrs. Cronk: "Almost unconsciously the women opened the hymnbooks they had just closed, to see the third stanza. Miss Sparkman read aloud the words of the omitted verse, on which the eyes of every member of the society rested,—

> Take my silver and my gold,
> Not a mite would I withhold.

" 'I am opposed to omitting the third verse,' said the little lady. 'If it were just in our singing it wouldn't be so bad, but we are omitting it in the life of our society. The amount of money that has come into our treasury this year is shamefully small. The appeals from our mission fields are read and we listen to them and say placidly, "How interesting," but we omit the third stanza.' "[2]

Miss Havergal was the author of a number of other hymns, prominent among which are "I Gave My Life for Thee," and "Tell It Out."

She died on the third of June, 1879, at the age of forty-two. At her request, the inscription upon her tombstone is from the First Epistle of John, "The blood of Jesus Christ his Son cleanseth us from all sin."

Few, if any, have left a greater impress upon the world for spirituality than she.

---

[1] Copyrighted by The Sunday School Times Company, and used by permission.

[2] Copyrighted by Missionary Review Publishing Company, and used by permission.

VII

THERE IS A FOUNTAIN

A sufferer from the effects of delirium tremens sat on a whiskey barrel in a New York saloon, lost in meditation. And he had much to meditate upon —a broken vow to his departed mother that he would never touch liquor; a profligate and wasted life; the experience of a gambler; and a recently broken-up home, which had been presided over by a loving and patient wife.

Suddenly he walked up to the bar, and pounded it until the glasses rattled. "Boys," he said to the loungers about him, "I am dying, but I will die in the street before I take another drink."

He made his way to the police station, and asked that he might be locked up, saying, "I want to be placed somewhere so I can die before I get another drink of whiskey." His request was granted and he was locked in a prison cell, but he was kindly treated. On the following Sunday, upon the advice of a friend, he went to the Jerry McAuley Cremorne Mission, where he found the chapel crowded with thieves, pickpockets, drunkards, and many men and women of evil life.

Jerry McAuley led in prayer. He was followed in earnest pleading by his wife, and then Jerry, while still kneeling, sang the hymn, "There Is a Fountain," beginning with the first verse, "There is a fountain filled with blood."

Samuel H. Hadley, in telling the story in *Down in Water Street*, says: "I had heard that dear old song years before, around our fireside at evening prayer, in my happy childhood, and it came back like a sweet memory. . . . Jerry's hand was on my head. He said: 'Brother, pray.' 'I can't pray, won't you pray for me?'

" 'All the prayers in the world won't save you unless you pray for yourself.' I halted but for a moment, and then with a breaking heart, I said: 'Dear Jesus, can you help me?'

"Never with mortal tongue can I describe that moment. Although up to that time, my soul had been filled with indescribable gloom, I felt the glorious brightness of the noonday sunshine in my heart. I felt that I was a free man. Oh, the precious feeling of safety, of freedom, of resting on Jesus! I felt that Christ with all his love and power had come into my life. From that moment until now, I have never wanted a drink, and have never seen money enough to make me take one. The precious touch of Jesus' cleansing blood in my soul took from my stomach, my brain, my blood, and my imagination, the hell-born desire for whiskey. Hallelujah! What a Saviour!"[1]

Mr. Hadley's faithful wife rejoined him, and, again they established a home. He obtained a remunerative position, but the call came to him to become Superintendent of the Water Street Mission. He accepted the position and held it for years, rendering faithful and consecrated service to the outcasts of the great metropolis.

The hymn, "There Is a Fountain," was written by William Cowper, and published in the *Olney Hymns* in 1779, although it was probably written sometime before this. It was entitled, "Praises for the Fountain Opened," and is based on the first

---

[1] From *Down in Water Street*, by Samuel H. Hadley. Copyrighted, and used by permission of Fleming H. Revell Company, publishers.

verse of the thirteenth chapter of Zechariah: "In that day there shall be a fountain opened to the house of David and to the inhabitants of Jerusalem for sin and for uncleanness."

William Cowper was born at Berkhamstead, Hertfordshire, England, on November 26, 1731, and died at East Durham, on April 25, 1800. He was the son of a clergyman, and was related to a number of prominent people. He was given splendid school opportunities; but his gentle and sensitive nature was greatly harassed by the rude and cruel treatment of his older schoolmates. He studied law for awhile, and then received an appointment to a government position; but he shrank from contact with the public, and declined the offer. He gave himself to literary pursuits, and wielded a pure and powerful pen. He was ever ready to defend the cause of the weak and oppressed.

A strong friendship sprang up between him and the preacher and poet, the Reverend John Newton. For a number of years, he lived in Mr. Newton's home. The hymns of both of these great poets appear in the *Olney Hymns*.

Mr. Cowper's life is one of the most tragic in hymnology. He was deprived of a mother's care by her death when he was only six years old. He was afflicted with melancholia, and at periods his reason would be entirely dethroned. Several times in these fits of insanity, he attempted suicide, but the hand of the Lord was upon him and restrained him.

These acts left him in great despondency, and in July, 1764, he was reading the Bible to find some relief from his despair, when he read from the twenty-fourth and twenty-fifth verses of the third chapter of Romans: "Being justified freely by his grace,

through the redemption that is in Christ Jesus:
whom God has set to be a propitiation through faith
in his blood, to declare his righteousness for the re-
mission of sins that are past, through the forbear-
ance of God."

Speaking of the effect of these verses upon his
soul, the poet says: "Immediately I received
strength to believe, and the full beams of the Sun
of Righteousness shone upon me. I saw the suf-
ficiency of the atonement Christ had made, my pardon in His blood, and the fullness and completeness
of His justification. In a moment I believed and
received the Gospel."

When the clear light of reason broke through
the clouds that often enveloped the poet, he would
take his pen, and write marvelously for the glory
of God, who had been his "shield and buckler."

The hymn appeals to the deepest sentiments of
the human soul. The wastrel in the slums realizes
the hold of sin upon his life, and the inability of
any human hand to draw him from the mire of
evil. And the handsomely gowned, and jewel be-
decked debutante upon the avenue realizes, if prop-
erly awakened to spiritual things, that silks and
broadcloth may cover but not eradicate a multitude
of sins. In the unlettered herdsman, and the cultured scholar, there is a need of the soul, that is not
met by the open spaces for the one, or man-made
philosophies for the other. In the convicted soul,
there is the cry for cleansing that can be given only
by the blood shed upon Calvary.

We read in Romans: "Much more then, being
now justified by his blood, we shall be saved from
wrath through him."

In 1 John, "And the blood of Jesus Christ his son
cleanseth us from all sin."

And in Revelation, "Unto him that loved us, and washed us from our sins in his own blood."

Perhaps no hymn has been sung under more somber circumstances than this one, as shown by an occurrence related by the Reverend William Taylor in *Seven Years' Street Preaching in San Francisco*. On a Sunday afternoon in June, 1856, Mr. Taylor was crying to the multitude on the street, "Be ye reconciled to God." Suddenly he noticed a great commotion, and he learned that the Vigilance Committee had arrested a desperado, and was taking him to the place of execution. A multitude gathered to witness the gruesome spectacle.

Mr. Taylor knew that, however much the criminal merited condign punishment, the members of the crowd were, themselves, polluted with iniquity. As the people came streaming back to their accustomed places, he took a favorable position, and sang "There Is a Fountain." He then preached an earnest sermon, laying upon the hearts of his hearers the burden of their own sins, and he pleaded with them to come to the fountain opened "for sin and uncleanness." Mr. Taylor says: "Good order and great seriousness prevailed. Eternity will reveal the fruit."

In *Anecdotes, Illustrative of New Testament Texts*, is the story of a robber, who had come under the conviction of sin, but who was despondent about salvation being for the likes of him. A Christian prayed with him, and sang the first verse of "There Is a Fountain." But the poor sinner said: "There is nothing in that for me." Then the Christian worker sang the second verse about the dying thief, and the man exclaimed: "That means me." And he accepted the Saviour as his Redeemer.

Dr. Charles L. Goodell, in *Followers of the Gleam,* relates this testimony concerning this hymn, as given by a former convict, who had been redeemed, and who was then holding a place of great trust in a banking institution.

The man said: "When I came out of prison the last time I made up my mind I would do differently. One night I went to church and heard about a chance for such men as I had been. The minister said that a man whose heart and hands had been stained with sin might yet be cleansed and his evil heart become tender and pure. That seemed too good to be true, and I thought there must be some mistake about it. But I went the next night and the night after, and he seemed so sure about it, and sang the old hymn,

> The dying thief rejoiced to see
> That fountain, in his day,
> And there may I, though vile as he,
> Wash all my sins away.

"You know what a thief I had been and I thought I knew something about that other thief and that seemed as if were written for me. So I went again and again, and at last the blessedness of it all came upon me like a great light, and I felt that I had lost all my old desires, and I had a new set of longings, and I hardly dared to go to sleep at night for fear they would slip away from me before morning. But my life was really changed."[1]

A drunken sailor, who had been discharged from the navy because of drunkenness, was making his way unsteadily along a New York street when suddenly music fell upon his ears. He had heard so-called music at the tawdry night club, and the ribald

---

[1]Copyrighted by Funk and Wagnalls. Used by permission.

song of the saloon dive, but this was different. It had a familiar sound. Yes, he had heard it often in childhood from his mother's lips, "There is a fountain filled with blood." He went into the room. It was the Jerry McAuley Mission on Water Street. He took a back seat, but when the invitation was given, he went forward, and confessed Christ; and John M. Wood, to his dying day, was a trophy of redeeming love. He was afterward appointed chaplain of the Navy Yard, perhaps its first unordained chaplain.

Militant Methodism quotes Bishop F. W. McDowell as saying to the first National Convention of Methodist men: "I would not cross the street to give India a new theology; India has more theology than it can understand. I would not cross the street to give China a new code of ethics; China has a vastly better ethical code, than ethical life. I would not cross the street to give Japan a new religious literature, for Japan has a better religious literature than religious life. But I would go around the world again, and yet again, if it pleased God, to tell India, and China, and Africa, and the rest of the world,

> There is a fountain filled with blood
>   Drawn from Immanuel's veins;
> And sinners, plunged beneath that flood,
>   Lose all their guilty stains."

This hymn is one among a number of hymns sung by the Bantus, for the African appreciates its sentiments as well as the European or American.

The hymn appeals to the saint of God, as well as to the unredeemed, for he knows that only through the blood of Jesus has cleansing come to his own soul. Dr. Newman Hall was with the sainted Cecil in his last hours, and they sang together, among other hymns, this great production.

William Cowper was not the voluminous producer of hymns as were some others who wrote their thousands. He is credited with only sixty-eight.

Dr. Jeremiah Bascom Reeves, in *The Hymn as Literature,* says that all of Cowper's piety and genius were not able to bring forth more than fifty lines of what might be pronounced great hymnody.

But Oh, What lines! What lines! Well may any individual covet to write just one line that will go ringing down the ages, calling men and women to God.

VIII

WHEN I SURVEY THE
WONDROUS CROSS

A young man, eighteen years old, was returning
from services in the Congregational Chapel in
Southampton, England, one Sunday, where his
poetic soul had been distressed by the crudity of the
music rendered, and he complained to his father,
who was one of the deacons, that the psalmnody in
use by the congregation did not measure up to the
true requirements of Christian worship.

"Then give us something better, young man," was
the somewhat sarcastic reply of the father.

Isaac Watts determined that he would under-
take that very task. On the following Sunday, he
arrived at the chapel with his first hymn, beginning,

> Behold the glories of the Lamb
> Amidst His Father's throne;
> Prepare new honors for His name,
> And songs before unknown.

The congregation sang the composition with great
earnestness, and asked for other hymns, which the
young man supplied week after week. Little did
they dream that this youthful poet was destined to
become one of the greatest hymn writers of all time.

Isaac Watts was the eldest son of nine children,
and was born on July 17, 1674, at Southampton,
England. His father, whose name was also Isaac,
was diligent in religious work, and was several
times arrested for this activity. At one time, he
spent six months in jail on account of his religion,
and was then compelled to leave the town for two

years. Time and again during her husband's imprisonment, Mrs. Watts, with her infant Isaac in her arms, would sit on a stone near the gate of the prison, and repeatedly hold the little fellow up to the window so that the father could see him.

The elder Watts afterward conducted a boarding school which won such a reputation that students attended from distant lands.

At an early age young Isaac developed a genius for verse making, and manifested his tendency in this direction by making so many rhymes that his father deemed it advisable to curb his youthful exuberance in this field. He threatened punishment if the boy did not discontinue this practice. However, Isaac's poetic fervor was so great that he could not desist, and his rhyming habit came into play even while he was being punished, for he exclaimed,

> Oh, father do some mercy take,
> And I will no more verses make.

It was a great thing for the world that the poetic gifts of this boy could not be stifled even by parental discipline; and the father decided to allow the youth to pursue his own selected course.

Young Watts was a studious youth and became noted for his learning. He entered the gospel ministry and preached his first sermon when he was twenty-four years old. After serving as assistant minister of the Mark Lane Independent Church, London, for awhile, he became regular pastor.

On account of impaired health, he accepted an invitation for a week's visit to the home of Sir Thomas and Lady Abney; and here, upon their insistence, he remained, making their residence his abode the remainder of his life which was nearly thirty-six years.

Dr. Watts was of small stature, being about five feet in height, and unpreposessing in appearance. He never married. He fell in love with Miss Elizabeth Singer, and she evidently, to some extent at least, reciprocated his affections. However, she said that she "loved the jewel, but could not admire the casket that contained it." Miss Singer married Professor Thomas Rowe, and attained some distinction as a poet.

Dr. Watts manifested great consideration for childhood. He wrote a number of poems for children, among them being that exquisite cradle song, "Hush, my dear, lie still and slumber."

He composed over six hundred hymns, among them being,

"Jesus Shall Reign"

"Joy to the World"

"Am I a Soldier of the Cross"

"O God, Our Help in Ages Past"

"Alas! and Did My Saviour Bleed?"

Dr. Charles S. Robinson says that, no doubt, more conversions have taken place during the singing of this last hymn than under any other in the English language.

Dr. Watts wrote not to achieve literary fame, but to give to the people verses through which they might voice the feeling of worshipful hearts.

As we look over the titles of our most frequently used and most effective hymns, we are impressed by the large number in this class that came from the pen of Dr. Watts, and of the elevating thoughts which they contain. He expresses himself in forceful but simple phrase. His words and sentiments are understood and appreciated by the unlettered as well as by the learned, for he spoke the universal language of the heart.

He wrote the profoundest truths and clothed them in language that appealed to the most cultured, but he used such clarity of expression that the humblest traveler along life's highway hears and understands the call to higher things. His hymns have an eminence of thought and a nobility of expression which awaken the most exalted feelings in the soul; and add to the loftiness and worshipfulness of any service in which they are used.

Perhaps no hymn is more forceful in creating an atmosphere of worship, and in fixing the minds of the congregation upon the sacrificial mission of Jesus Christ than the hymn, "When I Survey the Wondrous Cross."

At the meeting of the Southern Baptist Convention in Richmond, Virginia, in 1938, Dr. J. W. Storer, pastor of the First Baptist Church of Tulsa, Oklahoma, delivered an address on "The Dignity of Church Music." In his plea for ennobling and worshipful music in all our religious services, he related the following experience which occurred when he addressed a student convention in Gaffney, South Carolina, some years before.

Dr. Storer thus describes the incident: "The Sunday morning crowd was of course the largest, and not only the students but the townspeople crowded into the church. A young woman was the soloist. It was, so to speak, the 'show spot,' the opportunity of opportunities for exhibiting artistry and—self.

"The solo came just before the sermon. I remember I dreaded it. For my experience had prepared me for one of those heavy classical numbers which are supposedly necessary for implementing voice culture. But with the opening notes of the organ, I was at ease—at least the type of music would fittingly prepare the way for the sermon.

"Then the young woman began to sing—her voice a lovely contralto, moving, because of an evident inner experience— 'When I survey the wondrous cross, on which the Prince of glory died.' There was no parade of herself but, oh, such a pointing to him! I have heard many solos, but few that so moved me, and which had such an effect upon an audience. Our hearts were broken by the memory of His grace, before the sermon began. How easy it was to preach, how confidently the invitation given, and how rich was the response."

John B. Gough tells of attending with Dr. William M. Taylor, a meeting in Hoxton Hall, London, in one of the poorer and most abandoned quarters of the city. The services were conducted by a Mr. Noble. While on a visit to America, this gentleman had witnessed the work done by Jerry McAuley's Mission in New York City. He was so impressed that he determined to go back to England, and engage in similar missionary activity among the neglected classes.

Mr. Gough describes his experience in *Platform Echoes*: "Many of the audience were ragged and many of them were very poor, and the sight of them—numbering between twelve and fifteen hundred—was not particularly encouraging. Yet those meetings have been kept up regularly night after night, without intermission, and three times on Sunday, until nearly six hundred successive meetings have been held for these poor creatures in Hoxton Hall.

"The night Dr. Taylor was there with me, Mr. Noble said, 'Let us sing our favorite hymn,

> When I survey the wondrous cross
> On which the Prince of glory died,'

and they sang it with a will; and during the two minutes of silent prayer that followed you could hear their breathing."

H. Elvet Lewis, writing of the great revival which swept over Wales in the early part of this century, says that he heard this hymn sung in the meetings as he had never heard it before.

During the Torrey-Alexander meetings in Albert Hall, London, a number had declared their future allegiance to Christ, when Mr. Alexander said that instead of singing an entire hymn as usual, he would sing only one stanza, the third, of the noble hymn, "When I Survey the Wondrous Cross." And feelingly, he sang

> See from His head, His hands, His feet,
> Sorrow and love flow mingled down:
> Did e'er such love and sorrow meet,
> Or thorns compose so rich a crown?

When the invitation to confess Christ was given immediately following the hymn, about three hundred signified their acceptance of Jesus Christ as their Saviour.

During the meetings of these evangelists in Liverpool, one of the most notable conversions was that of Edward Roberts. He was a prize fight referee, and a thoroughgoing man of the world, but who, after his conversion, became a power for righteousness in his city.

Much against his wish, he accompanied his wife to the revival meetings, and on the following Monday, he greatly surprised her by announcing that he was going again to hear Dr. Torrey. The congregation sang that night "When I Survey the Wondrous Cross." Mr. Roberts says: "If I were to speak from now till tomorrow morning I could not describe the feeling that came over me when they sang that third verse. I got down and cried as I have never cried before or since. The love of Christ did it. I stood when the invitation was given and went to the front. I came out and went home and told my wife the glad news. She had been praying for me at home; and not until then did I learn that, together with a group of friends, she had been praying for my conversion for eight years."

Colonel Nicholas Smith relates in *Hymns Historically Famous*, the story of the conversion of James Delaney, who was a British artilleryman in India. He attended the preaching of the celebrated Baptist missionary, Eugenio Kincaid. In one of the services, in March, 1831, he heard for the first time the hymn, "When I Survey the Wondrous Cross." He had been a wild and reckless sinner, apparently insensible to any religious influence. But this hymn so touched his heart that he yielded to the Saviour's love, and became a changed man, and was baptized in the Salwin River.

When his term of service expired, he emigrated to the United States, and settled in Wisconsin in 1844. He became a Baptist minister; and, after a life of great usefulness died in 1896, at the age of ninety-three.

Rev. William H. Bates related these two incidents in *The Homiletic Review*, "Rev. John Watson tells us that when Matthew Arnold once attended his church, 'When I Survey the Wondrous Cross' was

sung.   Mr. Arnold left before the communion service that day.   As he came down the stairs in the
home where he was staying, a servant heard him
repeating this hymn.   At luncheon he spoke of it
and said that it was the finest hymn in the language.   (Soon after he went out and in ten minutes
he was dead.)

"On the ninetieth birthday of Professor Edwards
A. Park, sixty-eight years professor in the Andover
Theological Seminary, some two hundred of his
former pupils addressed to this great teacher letters
of congratulation.   Among the exercises in his home
that day, that which moved him most was the singing of 'When I Survey the Wondrous Cross.'   This
hymn, he said, he repeated oftenest to himself in
the sleepless night-watches."[1]

Dr. Watts died on November 25, 1748, at the age
of seventy-five, and was buried in Bunhill Fields, a
cemetery in London.   In addition to the tombstone
marking his last resting place, an imposing monument was also erected by voluntary subscriptions in
Southampton, the place where he was born.

---

[1]Copyrighted by Funk & Wagnalls Company, and used by permission.

IX

WHERE IS MY BOY TO-NIGHT?

Upon one occasion, when Ira D. Sankey was in Boston, Massachusetts, a lady who had heard that he was contemplating a journey across the continent asked him if he would try to find her wandering boy in California. This he consented to attempt.

He visited a number of cheap boardinghouses in search of the youth, and finally found him in the slums of the city. Mr. Sankey told him about the meetings which he was holding, and invited him to attend them. This he declined to do, saying that he was not fit to be seen at them. However, he was persuaded to attend. Mr. Sankey sang "Where Is My Boy Tonight?" prefacing the song with a statement that a mother in the East was praying for her wandering boy that very night. After the sermon the youth made his way to the inquiry room, and the singer experienced the great joy of leading him to Christ. Mr. Sankey wrote to the mother in Boston telling her of her son's conversion. She immediately sent money for his return home, where he obtained a position and became a useful follower of the Lord.

Many a wanderer from home and God has heard this appealing hymn and been awakened, and has been led to turn his feet into the paths that led both to his earthly home and to the heavenly home.

This hymn was written by Dr. Robert Lowry, who was born in Philadelphia, Pennsylvania, on March 12, 1826. He developed very early in life a fondness for music, and as a child delighted in getting his hands upon any musical instrument.

At the age of seventeen, he confessed his Saviour, and united with the First Baptist Church of Philadelphia. He began Christian work at once, taking an especial interest in Sunday schools. It was not long before he was impressed with the feeling that he should engage in the gospel ministry, and he entered Lewisburg, afterward Bucknell University, to prepare for his chosen calling.

He graduated with honors in 1854, and in the same year he was ordained, and became pastor of the First Baptist Church in West Chester, Pennsylvania. He also held pastorates with the Bloomingdale Baptist Church of New York City, and the Hanson Place Baptist Church of Brooklyn. He then returned to Lewisburg, where he became pastor of the Baptist church and professor in the college from which he had graduated. For some years after giving up the professorship, he was pastor of the First Baptist Church of Plainfield, New Jersey.

He traveled extensively in this country, and in Mexico and Europe. He was a great writer both of hymns and music. Among some of the most notable hymns for which he composed the music are "I Need Thee Every Hour," "The Mistakes of My Life," "All the Way My Saviour Leads Me," and "One More Day's Work for Jesus." Perhaps his own most noted compositions, for which he wrote both words and music, are "Shall We Gather at the River?" and "Where Is My Boy Tonight?"

He edited at least eighteen music books, millions of copies of which have been sold.

In *Twice Around the World With Alexander,* George T. B. Davis relates a touching incident concerning the singing of Dr. Lowry's hymn during the Torrey-Alexander meetings in Albert Hall, in

London. Mr. Alexander announced "Where Is My Boy Tonight?" The great audience joined heartily in the singing, and then the leader asked that just the fathers who had unsaved sons would sing the last stanza.

He said: "There may not be more than a dozen or two of you, but sing it if you have a son you would like to see saved. It doesn't matter if he is away off in China or India or where he is, the Lord can reach him." Mr. Davis describing the scene, says: "Then, not from a dozen, but from hundreds of throats, there arose in plaintive, pleading tones that brought tears to the eyes a subdued but strong volume of sound from the fathers in the audience who had wandering boys scattered far and wide over the face of the earth:

> Go for my wandering boy tonight,
>   Go, search for him where you will;
> And bring him to me with all his blight,
>   And tell him I love him still."[1]

One night during the meetings in Tasmania, Dr. Torrey asked Mr. Alexander to sing a solo. The singer was not expecting this request, but he hastily opened the hymnbook and sang this song. A poor fellow, under the influence of liquor, had wandered into the building and stood near the door in almost a drunken stupor. The sermon had made no impression upon his bewildered mind, and he seemed indifferent to the singing until the last verse of the hymn was reached. Then memory was awakened, manhood reasserted itself, and the man exclaimed: "That's for me." With contrite feelings he started down the aisle, went to the front and gave his heart to God.

Mr. Davis tells of an incident related by Mr. Alexander, which occurred in Dundee, Scotland. One night, when the singer was about to retire after a hard day's work, the hotel porter came to his room, and said that a gentleman wanted to see him. He tried to excuse himself, but the porter explained that the man insisted on seeing him at once.

Mr. Alexander then consented to go down, and thus describes the interview: "I went down and found a fine big Scotch farmer sobbing like a child. I said, 'What can I do for you? Are you a Christian man?' He said: 'I wasn't a Christian man until to-night, but I am now. I listened to Dr. Torrey's sermon, and withstood that and his appeal to come to Christ; but I was standing during the singing in the after-meeting, when the choir struck up the song, "Where Is My Boy Tonight?" I thought of my good old father who had gone to heaven three years before, and it touched my heart. Then at the close of the verse the choir sang "Tell Mother I'll Be There." My dear old mother had gone to heaven a little while before, and the memory of the home life and their sweet Christian lives was too much for me. I gave my heart to God and felt that I could not go home tonight until I had told you.' "

Ira D. Sankey said that the singing of the hymn, "Where Is My Boy Tonight?" has done more to bring back wandering boys than any other. He tells of a wayward boy who was brought to an evening service in Stanberry, Missouri, held by the Reverend J. H. Byers. The choir leader sang "Where Is My Boy Tonight?" This youth was converted and became a useful Christian worker. In their distant home, the parents of this boy were led to pray earnestly that day for their wayward son, and their hearts were gladdened by a telegram telling of his conversion.

In military camps, in mining camps, in lumber camps, the wandering boys themselves ask for the singing of this hymn. *The Missionary Review of the World* gives the story of the Reverend Dan Shultz, a pioneer missionary to the West. Upon one occasion, he was given the privilege of holding a meeting in a town hall just before the regular dance was to be held, but the fervor of his religious services threw a damper upon the subsequent festivities.

When Mr. Schultz asked if anyone present could play the organ, a man called out to a flashily dressed young woman: "Belle, show him what you can do." The preacher hesitated to accept her services, but as she had volunteered he decided to go ahead. She was a competent musician, and they sang several duets together. Then a cowboy called for "Where Is My Boy Tonight?" After the first stanza was sung the young organist broke down, hid her face in her hands and wept. The evangelist finished the song alone, and preached his sermon. The next day this young woman came to the minister, and told him that she had decided to lead a Christian life.

Rev. Thomas D. Whittles related, also in *The Missionary Review of the World,* an incident in the life of the Reverend D. K. Laurie, a missionary to the lumber camps of the Northwest. The minister took refuge from a storm one day in a shed where a camp cook was splitting wood. When the cook discovered that his visitor was a minister, he began to abuse the Christian religion, and remarked: "I tore up my Bible years ago." "Who gave you that Bible?" asked the preacher. "My mother," was the reply, and there came a marked change in the young man's demeanor.

Arrangements were made for services to be held that night. The cook was helpful and sang as a duet with the evangelist, "Where Is My Boy Tonight?" This young man was the son of a minister, but because of a disagreement with his father he had left home, and for seven years his people had not heard from him. However, through the influence of this song and the preaching of Mr. Laurie, this youth brought joy to his own heart and to his family by returning to them.

Perhaps no hymn voices more fully the uttered or unexpressed cry of the hearts of fathers and mothers sorrowing over wayward sons and daughters than does the hymn "Where Is My Boy Tonight?"

Mr. Sankey tells of a conversation between Chancellor Sims and a man whom he met on a train. When a boy this man had had a misunderstanding with his father, and had left his home in anger, vowing that he would never return. He had gone West and made a fortune, but had never written to his father since their separation. He was now on his way to his old home.

He gave this account of the circumstances that had led him to a change of heart: "A train on which I was traveling was snowed in, and people near by made up a load of provisions for the imprisoned passengers. It was discovered that Mr. Sankey was on board, and at the request of the passengers, he came out on the platform and sang 'Where Is My Boy Tonight?' That song touched my heart, led me to God, and I am now on my way East to seek a reconciliation with my parents."

David J. Beattie relates the following story in the *Romance of Sacred Song*. A lady was addressing a large audience in the Athenaeum at Bury, Lancashire, in England. At the close of her address, she made this announcement: "Before I came to Bury this afternoon, I made a call at Haslington to see a dear old woman. I told her I was coming and for why; then with tears in her eyes, she said, 'I wonder whether you can find my wandering boy?'"

Then followed the words of the stanza beginning, "Go for my wandering boy tonight." "I wonder," the speaker continued, "whether that wandering boy is here?"

"Yes," came a reply from the audience; and says Mr. Beattie, "From the back of the hall, through crowded aisles, a young man made his way to the front. Reaching forward the speaker grasped the outstretched hand, and after exchanging a few words, the lady raised her hand, and amid a tense silence said: 'Yes, it is that mother's boy. Do you wonder when I tell you that before I came away we knelt down in that cottage, and prayed that this boy might be found?' The prayer was answered. That night the wandering boy returned home."

Many other incidents could be given of the helpfulness of this soul-stirring hymn.

After a life of great usefulness as preacher, hymn writer, and music composer, Dr. Lowry died at Plainfield, New Jersey, on November 25, 1899, in the seventy-fourth year of his age.

X

ONWARD, CHRISTIAN SOLDIERS

War had broken out between two savage tribes on the Island of Tanna in the New Hebrides. It was being waged with diabolical cunning and cruelty, and might result in wiping out one tribe or both. The Reverend Frank L. Paton, the missionary on this island, was greatly distressed, and determined, even at the imminent risk of his own life, to prevent, if possible, the further spread of the conflict. He relates the story in *The Triumph of the Gospel in the New Hebrides.*

Gathering some of the Christians together, he went to the camp of one of the savage chiefs engaged in the conflict, and persuaded him to send some representatives to go with the company of Christians to the village of his enemy for a conference. As they crossed the battleground between the two camps, Mr. Paton and the converts from heathenism sang "Onward, Christian Soldiers." They were soldiers of peace and not of war. They bore no spear or battle-ax, and were protected by no man-made shield; but they were panoplied in heaven's armor, the helmet of salvation, the breastplate of righteousness, the shield of faith. They bore the sword of the Spirit and their feet were "shod with the preparation of the Gospel of Peace."

They won the victory, enemies shook hands, arms were laid aside, and there was great rejoicing, not only by Mr. Paton and his Christian helpers, but among the heathen themselves.

The hymn, "Onward, Christian Soldiers," was written by the Reverend Sabine Baring-Gould, and was published for the first time in 1865, in *The English Episcopal Church Times.*

Mr. Baring-Gould was born in Exeter, England, on January 28, 1834. He received an excellent education, graduating from Clare College, Oxford, in 1856, with the degree of M.A. He was ordained to the ministry in 1864, and became curate of Horbury.

He was a diligent writer, and over one hundred books are credited to his pen. He also wrote a number of hymns, the most noted being "Onward, Christian Soldiers" and "Now the Day Is Over." Speaking of his prodigious work, he said: "The secret is simply that I stick to a task when I begin it. It would never do to wait from day to day for some moments that might seem favorable for work.

At Horbury he fell in love with Miss Grace Taylor, whose family were in moderate circumstances, and both of them recognized the advisability of a better education for the young woman, if she were to become the wife of the minister in the community. With the consent of her parents, he sent her to college. Upon her return home the couple were married. She evidently was an especially gracious woman, as the union seems to have been a very happy one. At her passing, which was eight years before his own, Mr. Baring-Gould had inscribed upon her tomb, "Half of my soul." He died in 1924, at the age of ninety years.

In 1895, the author gave this account of the writing of his great hymn: "Whit-Sunday is a great day for school festivals in Yorkshire. On Whit-Monday, thirty years ago, it was arranged that our school should join forces with that of a neighboring village. I wanted the children to sing when marching from one village to another, but couldn't think of anything quite suitable; so I sat up all night, resolved that I would write something myself. 'Onward, Christian Soldiers' was the result. It was written in great haste, and I am afraid some of the rhymes are faulty. Certainly nothing has surprised me more than its popularity. I don't remember how it got printed first, but I know that very soon it found its way into several collections. I have written a few other hymns since, but only two or three have become at all well known."

"Onward, Christian Soldiers" is one of the most appropriate marching hymns for the Lord's redeemed while here on earth.

In 1806, several students of Williams College, Williamstown, Massachusetts, were accustomed to meet in a grove of maples near the institution. One evening a thunderstorm compelled them to take shelter under a haystack. They discussed the need of the heathen, earnest prayer was offered, and here the foreign missionary movement in America was born.

Ninety-one years after this haystack meeting, the World's Student Christian Federation met in Williamstown. One evening the delegates gathered around the memorial marking the spot where the haystack had stood, and reviewed the progress of Foreign Missions through the intervening years. There were delegates not only from America, but also from Europe, Asia, and Africa. As they marched away from this meeting, they sang in unison "Onward, Christian Soldiers."

The Reverend Neville Jones, a missionary to Africa, relates in *The Missionary Review of the World* how he called upon a drunken Matabele chief, named Guntu, and asked him to allow his family to attend the worship of God. The answer was an emphatic no. Some years afterward this savage was converted, and became so interested in the work of the Lord that he built for his people, at his own expense, a beautiful brick church. Mr. Jones describes the dedication of the church: "We gathered in the old pole and mud church building and after a hymn of praise and a prayer of deep thankfulness, we marched away to the new building headed by a choir of all the children present, singing 'Onward, Christian Soldiers.' On our arrival, the Reverend Shisho Moyo offered prayer and Guntu handed me the keys. I then opened the church to the glory of God."

Dr. H. Clay Trumbull gave an account, in *The Sunday School Times*, of the World's Sunday School Convention, held in Washington, D. C. in 1910. He says that at the closing session, after the opening services, a chorus of voices was heard in the distance, which increased more and more in volume until a group of sixty children came marching down the aisles singing "Onward, Christian Soldiers." And then the great audience present joined in with these children, and the spacious auditorium rang with this stirring hymn.

When the convention's meetings were held in Chicago, in 1914, a grand parade of Sunday school classes was held. Class after class, organization after organization, band after band passed along the street, and the hymn that was played or sung was almost invariably "Onward, Christian Soldiers."

During Mr. Sunday's meetings in Paterson, New Jersey, in 1915, the services one night were designated for the Junior Order of United American Mechanics, and forty-five hundred members of this order filed into the large tabernacle. As they approached, marching in line, the sound of the fife and the roll of the drum could be heard and then thousands of voices joined in singing this great marching hymn.

On May 23, 1903, the Knights Templars of the Grand Commandery of Pennsylvania paraded on Broad Street in Philadelphia. Forty bands with fifteen hundred musicians headed the procession followed by five thousand white-plumed knights. The great band played "Onward, Christian Soldiers," and the multitudes along the streets sang the hymn with great enthusiasm.

The Woman's Missionary Society of Utica, New York, adopted the following plan of welcoming new members. The president, holding a lighted candle, emphasized the necessity of enlisting the services of more messengers of light, and the committees who had secured new members came forward with them as the pianist played Mr. Baring-Gould's hymn.

Paolo was an Italian from America who was in Europe, representing an automobile firm during the World War of 1914-1918. He spent much of his time visiting hospitals and distributing Bibles. While visiting a base hospital, he found a wounded soldier who had lived in Cleveland, Ohio, who said: "Sing some America." Paolo sang "Onward, Christian Soldiers." In a letter written during the war, and published in *The Sunday School Times*, he thus describes the incident: "There are four verses. I sang them all. They then—three different men—asked me to repeat the refrain so that the men could catch it. I did so. That is, I taught it to them, and in no time they caught on and sung and sung it."

In 1913, a company of businessmen, headed by that great Sunday school leader, H. J. Heinz, visited different points in the Orient. In various places, the native Christians assembled to greet them, but the greatest gathering occurred at Seoul, Korea, where nearly fifteen thousand members of the Sunday schools came together on the parade grounds, and one of the songs they sung was this great marching hymn.

There was an evangelist who would not use this hymn in his meetings because he felt that it contained too much boasting. He would say: "We are a nice lot of soldiers!" And yet if we did not sing any hymn unless we fully lived up to its sentiments, there are a number in which we would not engage. However, there are many hymns that we can sing, not as a declaration that we have attained their conception of holiness, but as a profession that we are striving toward their ideal. Singing should not be simply words, words, and a tune, but it should be also the expression of the sincere worship of the heart. A hymn of praise should cause us more fully to adore our precious Lord; a hymn of consecration should draw us into closer fellowship with our Saviour; and a hymn of action, like "Onward, Christian Soldiers," should inspire us to more faithful effort in combating the forces of evil.

The Homiletic Review quotes from W. J. Howell in *The Christian Observer,* "During the recent Great War, there was evident everywhere the great importance our government attached to martial music. The soldiers were encouraged to sing, for a singing army is a conquering army; and the hearts of our men thrilled when they heard the inspiring strains of our national anthem. There are many who think the 'Marseillaise' is the grandest of all martial airs, and one can very well understand its

effect upon the French people when they are heard
to sing, 'Ye sons of France, awake to glory,' The
hymn, 'Onward, Christian Soldiers,' is the Marseillaise of the Christian soldier, and it would be a
fine thing if we could be emboldened by it to do
battle for our Lord and win victories of grace for
him."

Mr. Baring-Gould's hymn excites no hatred except the hatred for sin, and calls for no conflict except the conflict with evil. During the first World
War, some of the English soldiers supplanted "Tip-
perary" with "Onward, Christian Soldiers." The
substitution of the hymns of the cross for the hymns
of hate and bloodshed will hasten the coming of the
day of universal peace.

Dr. John Timothy Stone tells of the meeting of a
men's club in a local church, in which two hundred
eighty-five young men were present. The gathering
was addressed by General F. D. Grant, son of General U. S. Grant. Dr. Stone says: "When General
F. D. Grant began to speak, instinctively those men
drew their chairs up nearer about him. The meeting was intense in its informality. We were thrilled
by the spirit of the evening, and the loyalty of patriotism of these men.

"One among them was moved to say: 'Young
men, we not only need what our speaker has brought
to us, and that for which he stands, and for which
his honored father stood in our nation, but we need
a loyalty to Jesus Christ and to his standards.'
Those men rose up and sung one verse of 'My Country, 'Tis of Thee' for General Grant, and followed
with a verse of 'Onward, Christian Soldiers' for Jesus Christ. Their faces and voices spoke. We were
thrilled to our very hearts as we saw and heard

them. They sang with the loyal patriotism of young American manhood for our country, but they sang with equal enthusiasm for Jesus Christ."[1]

XI

THE DOXOLOGY

A visitor stood years ago at the entrance to a great copper mine in northern Michigan, waiting to see the day shift of miners come up from their work hundreds of feet below. Suddenly from the depths of the earth, he heard a jumbled sound of voices. Then they became clearer, and the words were distinguishable, "Nearer, My God, to Thee." The cage reached the mouth of the mine, the workmen stepped out, and with bared heads they sang "Praise God, from whom all blessings flow."

Perhaps no words ever written have been sung by more voices than this brief four-line doxology. These words are suitable for use in any pastime or occupation in which it is proper for the Christian to engage, and can be sung by rich and poor alike, upon any occasion, joyful or sad.

This Doxology was written by Thomas Ken, who was born at Birkhamstead, England, in July, 1637. He studied at Winchester School and at Oxford, and was ordained to the ministry about the year 1666. In 1679 he was appointed chaplain to Mary, Princess of Orange, and in 1680 he became chaplain to King Charles II.

He was a man of superior courage, and did not allow worldly interests to swerve him from the path of duty. In following the dictates of conscience, he sustained heavy financial losses, and was subjected to serious persecutions, being at one time imprisoned for his convictions.

Upon one occasion, Charles II visited the town in which Mr. Ken was ministering, and he was asked to entertain in his home some members of the king's retinue, notorious for their dissoluteness. He positively refused to comply with this request, saying that he would not do so "even for the king's kingdom." The king, instead of becoming incensed because of this attitude toward the royal favorites, evidently admired his independence, for some years after this, in 1684, he elevated Mr. Ken to the bishopric. He did not hesitate to speak to the king concerning his manner of life, and was his faithful spiritual adviser at the monarch's deathbed.

When William, Prince of Orange, became king of England as William III, Bishop Ken refused to repudiate his oath of allegiance, which he had previously given to King James, and on this account he was deprived of his high office and reduced to poverty.

Upon the accession of Queen Anne to the throne, she offered to restore him to his bishopric, but he declined, preferring to remain in retirement. The Queen, however, granted him a liberal pension, which enabled him to spend his declining days in comfort.

When he became conscious that the end of his life was near, he carefully examined his papers and destroyed those that might cause any bitterness after he was gone. He died at Longleat, Somersetshire, on March 19, 1711. He had requested that six of the poorest men in the parish should bear his body to its last resting place, and that he might be interred without any pomp "under the east window of the chancel, just at sunrising." This was done, and the sorrowing company sang one of Bishop

Ken's own hymns, "Awake, my soul, and with the sun."

Lord Macaulay, the great English historian, pays this tribute to his memory: "The moral character of Bishop Ken, when impartially reviewed, sustains a comparison with any in ecclesiastical history, and seems to approach, as near as any human infirmity permits, to the ideal of Christian perfection."

Dr. Ken used to sing his own compositions, accompanying himself on the lute. In addition to his other hymns he wrote three hymns, "Morning," "Evening," and "Midnight"; the last stanza of each hymn being the great Doxology; and these four lines have immortalized his name.

There are many things for which we can and should give thanks. There are unnumbered joys and privileges which come into our lives, to which we give no thought as gifts of the Heavenly Father, and for which no song of praise rings in our hearts.

Dr. Theodore L. Cuyler, the distinguished Brooklyn preacher, was visiting Charles H. Spurgeon in London. They spent a day in the country, roaming the fields with boyish glee. Mr. Cuyler related a story that greatly amused Mr. Spurgeon, and he laughed heartily. Then, turning suddenly to his visitor, he said: "Theodore, let's kneel down and thank God for laughter." And the two great men knelt under the trees upon a carpet of grass, and thanked God for the blessing of laughter.

We have but to look around us to find abundant cause for thanksgiving. Dr. Samuel W. Duffield, in his *English Hymns*, tells of a child who went with her father to the summit of Mount Washington. While they were above the clouds a thunderstorm rumbled below them. They stood in a narrow circle of almost bare rock, when the father said: "Well, Lucy, there is nothing to be seen here, is there?" But the child exclaimed: "O papa, I see the doxology. All around seems to say, 'Praise God, from whom all blessings flow.' "

The useful achievements of life should bring thankfulness to our hearts. Some years ago, a small group of visitors was standing in the compositor's room in the American Bible Society's building in New York. In the group was "a tall man, gray-haired, with pallid features." He and his wife were watching intently the printing that was being done. The man was the Reverend Hiram Bingham, D.D., who had gone years before as a missionary to the Gilbert Islands. He had reduced the speech of the natives to writing, had translated the Bible into that language, and now as he saw his dream of years come to pass in the printing of the Bible in that native tongue, tears trickled down his cheeks and he uttered a prayer of thankfulness to God. His companions lifted their voices in song, and the song was, "Praise God, from whom all blessings flow."

Dr. George C. Baldwin was pastor of the First Baptist Church of Troy, New York for forty-one years. On July 13, 1884, he preached the sermon of his fortieth anniversary. After recounting many of the mercies of the Lord, he paused and asked the congregation to stand and sing the Doxology. This they did, and the minister resumed his sermon.

Notwithstanding the great sacrifice which it entailed upon her, the mother of John Livingstone Nevius gladly gave him to mission work in China. In her old age, and far away from her beloved son, she dwelt almost in physical blindness, but glory, celestial, filled her soul, and she would be heard in the dark hours of the night singing "Praise God from whom all blessings flow."

Ira D. Sankey, in his *Story of the Gospel Hymns,* says that the first Moody and Sankey meeting held in the Agricultural Hall in London in 1874, was opened with the singing of the Doxology.

At the close of the Liverpool campaign sometime later, a large crowd gathered to bid Mr. Moody farewell, and, standing in the street in front of the hotel in which the evangelists were staying, they voiced their praises for the spiritual blessings which had come to their city by singing this great hymn.

George T. B. Davis, in *Twice Around the World With Alexander,* relates a number of instances in which the large audiences sang this hymn with great enthusiasm. At one time in a meeting in Liverpool, one hundred sixty men made public profession of their faith, and the audience rose spontaniously, and sang "Praise God from whom all blessings flow."

In 1905, the evangelist, Dr. R. A. Torrey, and the singer, Charles M. Alexander, conducted a notable evangelistic campaign in London, in which seventeen thousand people professed conversion. It was indeed fitting that at the close of the last service of these meetings, the great gathering, numbering thousands, should unite in singing Bishop Ken's Doxology.

"Billy" Dawson, a noted evangelist of the past century, preached at the opening of the Bridgehouse Wesleyan Chapel in Sheffield, England. The services were so inspiring that they continued all day and late into the night. As an expression of gratitude for the blessings that were being poured out, the

Doxology was sung during this meeting not less than thirty-five times.

Shah Jehan, one of India's powerful rulers, erected the Taj Mahal at Agra, India, as a tomb for his beloved wife, the Empress Moomtaj who died in 1631. This mausoleum is one of the most magnificent edifices in the world, and is described as a "poem in marble." The Empress was a bigoted Mohammedan, persecuting the Christians with an intense hatred. At her desire an inscription was placed upon the end of the tomb which faces the entrance, and which translated reads, "And defend us from the tribe of unbelievers." "Unbelievers" was a bitter term of contempt for Christians and all others who did not have faith in Mohammed.

Dr. William Butler, a distinguished missionary of the Methodist Episcopal Church, visited the Taj Mahal in 1856, and had this to say of the inscription: "Heaven would not answer the fanatical prayer of this mistaken woman; but, instead, has placed even her shrine in the custody of those she hated; and that very 'tribe' now gather from all parts of the civilized world, to enter freely and admire the splendors of the tomb which was raised over her remains, and smile with pity at the impotent bigotry which asked heaven to forbid their approach. The writer had the privilege, with a band of Christian missionaries, of standing around her tomb, and, in the presence of these words, of joining heartily in singing the Christian Doxology, while the echo above sweetly repeated the praise to 'Father, Son, and Holy Ghost.' "

In 1856, a company, with Mr. Cyrus W. Field as the moving spirit, was formed for the purpose of laying a telegraph cable across the Atlantic Ocean—

an accomplishment seemingly impossible, and ridiculed by many people. After failure in 1857 the cable was successfully laid in 1858, but after a few messages between the continents, the line became silent. It was not until after the Civil War that a satisfactory cable was laid, and instantaneous and regular communication between America and Europe was established.

The cable of 1858, while operating only a brief time, nevertheless, demonstrated the soundness of the proposition, and was a genuine cause for thanksgiving. Dr. Silas H. Paine tells us that·a thousand guests were seated at a collegiate dinner table in Andover, Massachusetts, when the news was conveyed of the sending of the first message across the ocean. The whole company arose and sang "Praise God from whom all blessings flow."

Perhaps the Doxology is not thought of very often as a funeral hymn, and yet when a consecrated life has closed, what more appropriate could be sung than these words of thankfulness for the life that has been lived. This brief hymn was one of the hymns sung at the funeral of the Reverend Mark Guy Pearse, whose ministry in England was so greatly blessed. He gave these instructions to a brother minister concerning arrangements for his funeral: "There must be no mourning, no tears, no misery, no gloom. I go not into the gloom but into the dawn. Start the service with 'Praise God.' Take all the stops out of the organ and let everybody thunder it out."

It would be well for the sentiment of this Doxology to permeate our daily living. It would give us joy and courage. At one time Dr. Henry W. Frost, of the China Inland Mission, was in a period of great spiritual depression. Entering a mission house, he saw this motto on the wall, "Try Thanksgiving." He followed its injunction and peace came to his soul.

In the cool of the morning hour, or when the sun's rays beat pitilessly at noonday, or in the darkness of midnight moments, the Lord's people can sing "Praise God from whom all blessings flow."

XII

ROCK OF AGES

A shabbily dressed and unkempt man shambled along a narrow New York street, of unsavory reputation. His former acquaintances would not have recognized in him the once prosperous businessman, that he had formerly been. Employees had willingly obeyed his commands, prominent businessmen had valued his friendship, and sought his counsel, and when the work of a busy day was over, a comfortable and luxurious home awaited him with its comforts and delights.

Financial disaster, however, overtook him. His fortune was swept away, disappointment overwhelmed him, and despair gripped his soul. Instead of putting his trust in God and struggling to regain a foothold in the business world, he surrendered to his reverses, and gave himself to drink and a life of dissipation. Penniless, friendless, and hopeless, he shuffled along the street. What was the use of further struggles? Why not end his miserable existence? And the horrible thought of self destruction came into his mind.

Suddenly he stopped and listened, not to the clang of an ambulance gong, or the siren of a fire engine, or the shrill call of a policeman's whistle, but to a song coming from a mission hall, and he heard the words of the hymn, "Rock of Ages." The words awakened a train of memories in his mind. He thought of father and mother and the boyhood home where this song had been often sung. Hesitantly he entered the hall, and took his seat. As he sat there, new hopes and new resolves came into his heart, and when he left that room he was a new man in Christ Jesus, ready to battle temptation and sin with fortitude and faith.

Outside the sacred Scriptures, few productions of the human pen have been more widely read and used than the hymn, "Rock of Ages." It was written by Augustus Montague Toplady, who was born at Farnham, Surrey, England, on November 4, 1740. When sixteen years old, while visiting relatives in Ireland, he attended an evangelistic service which was being held in a barn, and was converted. A Mr. Morris, unlettered, but a man of spiritual power, conducted the services, and preached from the thirteenth verse of the second chapter of Ephesians, "But now in Christ Jesus ye who sometimes were far off are made nigh by the blood of Christ."

Mr. Toplady was educated at Westminister School and Trinity College, Dublin, and received orders in the Church of England at the age of twenty-two. His ministry, for a while, was at a place called Broad Hembury, in Devonshire. Then at the age of twenty-eight, he was transferred to London. He was never physically strong, and in the early thirties, his health began to fail, and he died on August 7, 1778, at the age of thirty-eight.

Mr. Toplady was the editor of *The Gospel Magazine*, and besides numerous other writings he wrote a number of hymns. He would have been quickly forgotten, perhaps, if it had not been for the hymn, "Rock of Ages." By this one effort, brief as was his career, he won an enduring name for himself, and made an indelible impression upon the world. The hymn was first published in *The Gospel Magazine*, in 1776, a year memorable in American history. Its comforting and ennobling sentiments appealed at once to the multitude, and the production took an enduring place in Christian literature.

It is said that the occasion for the writing of the hymn came about in this way. One afternoon Mr. Toplady was out walking, when he was overtaken by a sudden thundershower, and took refuge in the cleft of a great rock. As the thunders rolled above him, and the storm raged around him, he realized the safety of his retreat. Then he thought of the storms of life that buffeted him, and of the fact that Jesus Christ was his sure refuge against the ills of human experience, and the words of the hymn came to him.

Many incidents are related concerning the strength and comfort which this hymn has given to people in all walks of life, and under varying circumstances. King and peasant, rich man and pauper alike, find consolation in its sentiments.

The British Weekly tells of a student who spent his vacation among the workmen who were building a railroad in Canada. Having won their friendship, he invited them to a religious service, and a large crowd came. Many of his auditors were rough and godless; but when asked that someone would suggest his mother's favorite hymn, "Rock of Ages" was called for. It was sung with heartiness time and again; and a number felt a spiritual influence that night.

Not only did it touch the lives of the lumberjacks of the Northwest, but it impressed with equal power the hearts of royalty. It was the favorite hymn of Queen Victoria, and also of her husband, Prince Albert, who repeated its words in his dying moments.

In the *Story of the Hymns and Tunes,* by Brown and Butterworth, there is related a pleasing story of the Queen's Golden Jubilee. One of the dignitaries presented to the Queen was an official from Madagascar. He astounded the court attendants by asking the privilege of singing at the interview. As novel as was the experience, they did not wish to offend this foreign dignitary, and so the request was granted. The Queen was greatly pleased, when this native of a country, so recently steeped in heathenism, sang "Rock of Ages."

This hymn was a favorite of Charles H. Spurgeon, and he often quoted from it in his sermons. When a youth, about sixteen years old, during a slight illness, he wrote in his diary a verse from this hymn changing two words; "Not well; the body bears the soul down. If I were long to be so heavy as I am now, I could scarcely live. Evening; could not attend to the sermon. I feasted all the time on,

> When I soar to worlds unknown,
> See Thee on Thy judgment throne,
> Rock of Ages, cleft for me,
> Let me hide myself in Thee."

The following incident was also related by Mr. Spurgeon. One of his colporteurs met a woman who had drifted far from God, but who had been brought under the conviction of sin, and was almost in a despairing condition. He supplied her with one of Mr. Spurgeon's sermons on "The Gentleness of Jesus." On the next day, the colporteur met her again; and, holding the sermon in her hand, and with radiant countenance, she exclaimed: "Blessed be the Lord forevermore, I have found Him, or rather He has found me. I am saved, pardoned, forgiven, accepted and blessed for Christ's sake. Now I know what the fact means,

> Nothing in my hand I bring,
> Simply to Thy cross I cling.

"Yes, yes, Jesus died for me, and I live through Him."

Miss Belle M. Brain related the following story in *The Missionary Review of the World:* Mrs. Lucy S. Bainbridge, who with her husband made a tour of the world studying Christian missions many years ago, tells of seeing a woman, who, to make merit, dug with her own hands a well twenty-five feet deep and from ten to fifteen feet across. Not until long after it was completed did she learn of free salvation through Christ.

"When Mrs. Bainbridge saw her, she was an old woman past eighty, but she stretched forth the old, crippled hands that had performed such incredible labor in a vain endeavor to save her soul, and sang with her visitor,

> Nothing in my hand I bring,
> Simply to Thy cross I cling."

The Sunday School Times gives the following incident, which was reported by Mr. Albert Orsborn, of Toronto, Canada: "The Rev. Joseph W. Kemp, in a sermon at Toronto, May 20, 1917, told of a letter received from a friend engaged in nursing wounded soldiers, in which the case of a young man was revealed who was told by the surgeons one day that an operation would be necessary in order to save his life; and so serious was the operation that in its performance, his power of speech would be completely destroyed.

"The young man resigned himself to the sad news, and requested permission to use his voice once more. The request was granted, and stepping out in the middle of the hospital ward, his voice, which had been so often used in the Saviour's service before, rang out his last song,

> Rock of Ages, cleft for me,
> Let me hide myself in Thee."

Miss Frances E. Willard, in her autobiography, *Glimpses of Fifty Years,* describes her visit with a party of friends to the pyramid of Cheops, on the banks of the Nile. They stood in the inner chamber which held the great sarcophagus, and sang "Rock of Ages, cleft for me."

Miss Willard says: "With swelling hearts we joined in the dear old hymn, 'Rock of Ages, cleft for me,' we learned so long ago, so far away. At its close, solemn and deep sounded the voice of Dr. Park, our leader; I shall not soon forget the words: 'The pyramids may crumble, but the Rock of Ages stands firm and secure. The old idolatry that reared this awful tomb has had its long, its little day. The kingdom of our Lord and of His Christ is ushered in, and we, His ransomed sons and daughters, sing of Him who hath so loved us, standing in the empty coffin of the idolatrous and cruel Pharaoh.' "[1]

And continues Miss Willard: "Let Egypt boast her mystic monuments, which, in the race with time, have come off grimly victorious; a Christian's eye pierces the boundless blue above their heads, and gets a glimpse of more enduring habitations, while, as he turns away from their pitiless masses

[1]Copyrighted by The Woman's Temperance Publication Association 1889, and used by permission.

of stone, his humble, happy faith sings of the 'Rock
of Ages, cleft for me."

This was one of the hymns sung at the funeral
of this great temperance leader.

General J. E. B. Stuart, that able Confederate
cavalry commander, was mortally wounded at Yel-
low Tavern, in the fighting around Richmond. He
was taken to a hospital in the city, and it is said
that before he died he asked that "Rock of Ages"
be sung to him.

It is recorded that a company of Armenian Christians in Constantinople, some years ago, sang this
hymn as they were being martyred for their faith
by the cruel Turks.

As the steamer London was sinking in the Bay
of Biscay, in 1886, a group of passengers stood
upon the deck, and sang "Rock of Ages," as they
went down into a watery grave.

The story of the wreck of the steamer *Seawan-
haka,* loses none of its thrill in its oft repeating. A
number of the passengers who had escaped from
the doomed vessel were struggling in the water,
clinging to life preservers and portions of the ship.
Lifeboats began picking up the survivors as rapidly as possible, but it was slow work. A singer
and his wife were holding desperately to the same
piece of wreckage, hoping and waiting for the life-
boat.

Finally the young wife said: "I can hold on no
longer." "Try a little longer," urged her husband,
"and let us sing 'Rock of Ages.'" These notes of
hope floated over the darkened waters, and one by
one others who were despairing and about to give
up the struggle caught up the song, which inspired

physical strength and spiritual courage, and their lives were saved.

Some years ago, ten thousand people gathered on the spot where tradition says that this hymn was written, to honor the memory of the author.

The publishers of an English periodical asked their readers to select the one hundred English hymns that stood highest in their estimation. Of thirty-five hundred persons who responded, three thousand three hundred fifteen of them gave this hymn the first place on their lists.

Dr. S. D. Gordon named this hymn as the favorite of the Christian life, and someone has said that it is "the best known, best loved, and most widely useful hymn in the English language."

XIII

MY FAITH LOOKS UP TO THEE

An unconverted young man had been in the habit of attending preaching at the First Congregational Church of Albany, New York, of which Dr. Ray Palmer was the pastor. One Sunday he took his seat, and while waiting for the services to commence he began looking through the hymnbook. His attention was attracted to the hymn, "My Faith Looks Up to Thee." He read a few lines, which proved to be a message to his own heart, that led him to Jesus. He afterward called at the residence of Dr. Palmer to tell him about his conversion, and was surprised and pleased to learn that that minister himself was the author of the hymn that had so greatly impressed him.

Dr. Palmer was the son of Honorable Thomas Palmer, and was born at Little Compton, Rhode Island, on November 12, 1808. The foundation of his education was laid in the teaching in his own home, but at the age of thirteen he was earning his living by clerking in a dry goods store in Boston, Massachusetts.

Dr. Samuel W. Duffield says in *English Hymns:* "The lives of the English hymn-writers, as a rule, show the presence of wealth and culture; those of Americans—as a rule—show the presence and pressure of poverty and hard surroundings. In Dr. Palmer's case this rule was unaltered."

Young Palmer united with the Park Street Congregational Church, and soon felt the call to become a preacher of the gospel. He took a three years' course at Phillips Academy, Andover. He then entered Yale, graduating in 1830. For a short while, he taught in a school for young ladies in New York City, and it was at this time that his immortal hymn was written.

He then pursued the study of theology, and in 1835 he was ordained to the gospel ministry, and became pastor of the Central Congregational Church of Bath, Maine. He also held pastorates in Albany, New York, and in Newark, New Jersey. For thirteen years he was secretary of the American Congregational Union, and for a while he resided in New York City.

Dr. Palmer wrote a number of hymns—in fact, two volumes; but the one that stands out pre-eminent among them, and holding a place of honor among the world's great hymns, is "My Faith Looks Up to Thee."

This hymn was written in 1830, when Dr. Palmer was only twenty-two years old. So deep were the young man's spiritual feelings while writing these lines, that he gave way to copious tears as he penned the last words.

The poem was written first on loose sheets of paper, and then copied into a little morocco covered book which the author was accustomed to carry with him for just such notes. It was not written to be sung as a hymn, or even for publication, but simply as an expression of the author's sentiments.

About two years after he had written it, Dr. Lowell Mason, the noted music composer, met him on the street in Boston and asked him to furnish some hymns for a collection which he was compiling. Mr. Palmer showed him the hymn, and gave him a copy of it. Mr. Mason took it home, and composed for it the tune, "Olivet."

Meeting the author a few days afterward, he exclaimed: "Mr. Palmer you may live many years and do many good things, but I think you will be best known to posterity as the author of 'My Faith Looks Up to Thee.'" It was a prophecy which the popularity of the hymn has fully justified.

This poem comprehends life's needs, and becomes a satisfying prayer for the human soul as few hymns have ever done. Bishop Edwin H. Hughes tells of attending a service, in which a prominent minister was asked to lead in prayer, and he began with the words, "My faith looks up to Thee," and his entire prayer consisted of this poem.

Many have heard this hymn and, realizing that their faith did not look up to God, have, under its inspiration, turned unto the Lord.

A businessman residing in New York State consulted a physician in New York City concerning his health, and was shocked to learn that he would live probably no longer than six months. Before returning home, he visited a friend, an earnest Christian woman, who spoke helpful words to him, and placed a printed leaflet in his hand. While on the train he thought of the leaflet which was in his pocket and began to read it. It contained the hymn, "My Faith Looks Up to Thee." Business affairs had so occupied his mind that he had given but scant attention to the interests of his soul. But this hymn pointed him to the Saviour, and his last few months were spent in joyful service of the Master.

Mr. Allan Sutherland, in *Famous Hymns of the World*, tells of the conversion of the world's champion clog dancer, Mike Riley, who had been mastered by drink. On a winter night, penniless and homeless, he had started to the river to end his miserable existence, when he was attracted by the warm glow of the Bowery Mission. He entered, as he expressed it, "just to get warm once more before ending it all in the river."

The hymn, "My Faith Looks Up to Thee," was being sung. The words appealed to the wanderer, and he realized that the river would bring no surcease to his troubled soul; and that the blood of Jesus, shed for him and all like him, was the only remedy for sin. He left the room a redeemed man, and, instead of ending his life that night, he spent the rest of his days winning sinning men to the Redeemer.

This hymn is full of comfort and strength for sorrowing and weary travelers along life's road. Dr. Sheldon Jackson, that great missionary to Alaska, said: "For my own personal comfort, I have found that 'My Faith Looks Up to Thee' has given me the most of comfort and strength."

A young woman, who had been a great sufferer, tells of awaking one morning with a feeling of depression and great discouragement. The rain was beating against the window panes, and the dreariness of the day was echoed in her own heart. Suddenly she heard the sound of music, and she realized that the family, not wishing to disturb her, had gathered in another part of the house for morning worship. The strains of "My Faith Looks Up to Thee," came to her; and although the clouds still hung heavy over the city, the glory of the divine Presence filled her soul.

In 1852, Mr. D. L. Moody was returning to America on the steamer *Spree*, from a great evangelistic campaign in Great Britain. When at sea several days the propeller shaft of the ship broke, and the vessel was driven helplessly before the storm. Death in a watery grave momentarily threatened the more than seven hundred men and women on board. Finally a rescuing steamer, *The Lake Huron*, came in sight. At the height of the danger, a religious service was held in the saloon of the vessel, and so rough was the sea that Mr. Moody had to hold firmly to a pillar, while he read the ninety-first Psalm, and passages from the one hundred seventh Psalm. Jews, Protestants, Catholics, and skeptics gathered for the service, and several hymns were sung, among them being "My Faith Looks Up to Thee."

Few hymns appeal more to the Christian soldier, compelled to face death upon the battlefield, than does this one. Dr. Palmer, in the appendix to his *Poetical Works*, tells of a group of six or eight Christian young men, who met together in one of their tents on the evening before an expected battle, which proved to be one of the fiercest of the Civil War. After spending some time in prayer and religious conversation, they decided to draw up and sign a statement of faith and assurance to leave for their loved ones in case they did not return from the conflict. After some discussion, it was unanimously agreed that the hymn, "My Faith Looks Up to Thee," should be written out, and signed by each one as an evidence of their unshaken faith in God in that trying hour. Several of these brave youths fell in the battle of the next day.

In *The Beautiful Life of Frances E. Willard*, by Miss Anna A. Gordon, is this story of the battle of Seven Pines. In one of the New England regiments engaged in that struggle, every member was a professed Christian, even the members of the brass band. In the forefront of the battle, and subjected to a withering fire, they were driven back and retreated into the forest. The colonel called on the band to play one of their favorite hymns of boyhood days, "My Faith Looks Up to Thee," and, under the inspiration of this hymn, and notwithstanding the final outcome of the battle, they won glory for their command.

Around the world, men and women have lifted up their hearts to God in this hymn as it has been translated into a number of languages.

Dr. Henry Jessup, a well-known missionary to Syria, sent a message to the author of this hymn: "Tell Dr. Palmer that as I write I hear a hundred and twenty Mohammedan girls singing "My Faith Looks Up to Thee."

Mrs. E. R. Pitman, in *Missionary Heroines in Eastern Lands*, tells of an old Syrian woman who was nearing her journey's end, and growing more feeble every day. The missionary asked her if she knew the hymn, "Just As I Am." Her face brightened, and she joined her daughter and the missionary in singing it. Then she said: "But there is one hymn that I like better." And she sang with wavering voice "My Faith Looks Up to Thee."

Mr. Philip E. Howard, writing in *The Sunday School Times*, about some experiences while attending the World Sunday School Convention in Rome, Italy, in 1907, gives this account of a visit to the catacombs, those wonderful underground passages, where the early Christians buried their dead; and where they, themselves, hid away from their persecutors, and worshiped the living God. The little company from far-off America gathered there in the gloom of these man-made caverns, offered prayer, and sang "My Faith Looks Up to Thee."

Dr. Theodore L. Cuyler, in his *Recollections of a Long Life,"* says: "By common consent, in all American hymnology this hymn is the best."

Dr. Cuyler relates the following: "Dr. Palmer preached several times in my Brooklyn pulpit. He was once with us on a sacramental Sabbath. While the deacons were passing the elements among the congregation the dear old man broke out in a tremulous voice, and sang his own heavenly lines,

> My faith looks up to Thee,
> Thou Lamb of Calvary,
> Saviour divine.

"It was like listening to a rehearsal from the celestial choir, and the whole assembly was most deeply moved. Dr. Palmer was short in stature, but his erect form and habit of brushing his hair high over his forehead gave him a commanding look. He was the impersonation of genuine enthusiasm. Some of his letters I shall always prize. He fell asleep just before he reached a round fourscore, and of our many hymn-writers no one has yet 'taken away his crown.' "[1]

Dr. Palmer died in Newark, New Jersey, on March 29, 1887. In his pastoral visits, it had been his custom to recite his own hymns to the sorrowing and suffering. On the day before he passed into the great beyond, the comfort of one of those same hymns was his, for he was heard to murmur as his last words:

> When death these mortal eyes shall seal
> And still this throbbing heart,
> The rending vail shall Thee reveal
> All glorious as Thou art.

---

[1]From *Recollections of a Long Life,* by Theodore L. Cuyler. Copyrighted by Fleming H. Revell Company, publishers, and used by permission.

XIV

NEARER, MY GOD, TO THEE

A prisoner, named Benjamin Flower, sat behind the bars of an English jail. This was not a pleasant experience, but he was not a felon. He had committed no crime for which he should be thrust into a prison cell. He was the editor of the *Cambridge Intelligencer,* and had expressed some opinions in an article which were not in accord with those of the rulers of his day, and he had been arrested.

Some ladies, who sympathized with him in his plight, were permitted to visit him in the prison, and among them was a Miss Elza Gould. An attachment sprang up between the two, and sometime after Mr. Flower gained his liberty, he and his fair visitor were united in marriage.

One of the children of this couple was named Sarah, and was born at Harlow, England, on February 22, 1805. She developed a talent for poetry, and wrote several hymns. She married John Brydges Adams in 1834, and about the year 1840, she wrote the immortal hymn, "Nearer, My God, to Thee." She died in 1848.

The hymn is based on Jacob's experience as he fled from the wrath of his brother Esau, after he had swindled that brother out of the patriarchal blessing through deceiving his blind old father. No doubt remorse had already overtaken the fugitive, and his heart was in distress because of separation, it may be for the first time, from a lenient and doting mother. Perhaps he felt also that he was leaving the sovereignty of his father's God. Although he worshiped the living God, he, evidently, shared the belief of his heathen neighbors that the power of Jehovah was confined to the limits of a restricted locality. Here at Bethel, he learned that God was still near him, and while he might run away from his home, and his native land, he could not run away from the presence of the Heavenly Father.

In the hymn we see the sun going down upon the wanderer and darkness enveloping him; and as he rests with his head upon a stone, a heavenly dream comes into his troubled slumbers. He sees the angels ascending and descending upon the ladder let down from the gates of heaven, and he hears the voice of God, saying: "And, behold, I am with thee in all places whither thou goest."

Waking from his sleep after this night of vision, the fugitive exclaims: "Surely the Lord is in this place, and I knew it not." And he goes on his way with the sentiment of this poem echoing in his heart, to be expressed centuries afterward by Mrs. Adams in "Nearer, My God, to Thee."

Perhaps no hymn has been sung more often, or in a greater number of places, or under more varied circumstances than this one.

If it had been in existence, it could have been sung at the marriage feast in Cana of Galilee, which Jesus graced by his presence, adding joy to the occasion. And it could have been sung with equal appropriateness in the home where the angel of death had laid his cold hand upon the little daughter of Jairus, the ruler of the synagogue.

It can be sung in the home of deepest grief, bringing comfort to broken hearts; and its use need not, in the least, dampen the enthusiasm of youthful spirits, engaged in wholesome diversion.

From yonder tower the chimes peal out its melody o'er hurrying and busy crowds, striking a responsive chord in many a heart. In gladsome tone the children sing its words in home and on crowded street. And the wavering voice of old age pours forth its notes.

Few people would make a list of favorite hymns, without including this one. When the mother of Lady Henry Somerset decided to present Miss Frances E. Willard with a music box, she asked the great temperance leader what music she preferred in it. Miss Willard replied, "The hymns that mother loved best." We are not surprised to learn that among them was "Nearer, My God, to Thee."

At a summer institute, attended by a number of young people, they were asked to vote upon what they considered the best ten hymns, and Mrs. Adams' hymn was in the list.

At the Foreign Missions Convention in Washington, D. C., in 1925, Dr. E. H. Richards, for a number of years a missionary to Africa, told about teaching the natives to sing "Nearer, My God, to Thee," and of the widespread popularity it attained along with other hymns.

Mr. J. H. Morrison, in *Streams in the Desert*, speaks of the singing around missionary campfires on missionary journeys in Africa, and says: "The sacred and familiar music of 'Rock of Ages,' 'Nearer, My God, to Thee,' and the 'Sweet By and By,' wedded to strange words, and sung in that far-off land, fell on the ear with singular pathos, and sent surges of feeling through the heart."

Mrs. James Chalmers, who shared with her husband the hardships and dangers of missionary life among the savages of the South Sea Islands, tells in her journal of teaching the native boys to sing this hymn in their own language.

Some years ago, *The Missionary Review of the World* gave a translation of "Nearer, My God, to Thee," made into the Eskimo language. The translation was made by the Reverend John Kilbuck, who was a full-blooded Indian of the Delaware tribe, great grandson of the famous chief Gelelemend. The chief was converted and became an earnest worker in the Moravian Church. The grandson followed in his steps, and not only became a devoted Christian, but a missionary to the Eskimos.

And so we find this hymn appealing to every race and every clime, expressing the desire of each true disciple to be nearer to his Lord. Of course, it has been translated into a number of other languages.

Many are the instances recorded of the power of this hymn over human hearts. In the *History of the Hymns and Tunes,* by Theron Brown and Hezekiah Butterworth, it is related how a forger was brought under conviction and to repentance by hearing the singing of this hymn. Eight years before, he had committed a forgery in the city of Boston, Massachusetts, and since that time he had been a fugitive from Justice.

On a Sunday in November, he was in Pittsburgh, Pennsylvania, lonely, despondent, and harassed by recollections of a wasted past and ruined present. He stepped into a theater where a religious service was being held, hoping that the music might divert his thoughts. "Nearer, My God, to Thee" was among the hymns that were being sung. The words awakened the memory of those days when he walked the streets of his city an upright and respected citizen. He felt a desire to draw near to that God whose laws he had trampled beneath his feet. Tears were falling upon his cheeks as he left the building. Sleep fled from his eyes, and in anguish he paced the floor of his bedroom all night. The next morning he confessed his crime to the police, surrendered to them and was taken back to Boston.

This hymn was a favorite of President Theodore Roosevelt, and it carried him back to the days when he led his Rough Riders in their furious charges in Cuba during the Spanish-American War; for time and again it was sung by his soldiers as they laid to rest some fallen comrade.

President William McKinley was a lover of song, and often his rich voice could be heard as it mingled with others in the singing of the services which he attended. Struck down on September 6, 1901, by the hand of an assassin, his noble earthly career was abruptly ended, for he died eight days later on September 14. As he was passing into the shadows of the valley, he sang with waning voice, "Nearer, My God, to Thee." On the day of his funeral in Canton, Ohio, nearly all the machinery in the United States, including that which operated trolley cars and trains, was stopped for five minutes, and in nearly every church in the land was sung "Nearer, My God, to Thee." The heart of a nation was lifted nearer Jehovah as the people thought of the passing of this great Christian statesman.

In many humble homes, where the name of the voyager into the beyond is unknown to fame, this hymn has shed its radiance. A little drummer boy at Fort Donelson, during the Civil War, was found mortally wounded upon the field of battle, but he was singing with his remaining strength the words of this great hymn.

Thousands of Armenians were massacred in Turkey in the early part of this century because of their Christian faith. A group of college boys were led out by the officers to the place of execution. Their request to sing was granted, and their last message to the world was in the hymn "Nearer, My God, to Thee."

On April 10, 1912, the greatest ship afloat sailed out of Southampton Harbor, in England. The ship was so constructed as to be considered unsinkable. The names of many wealthy and distinguished individuals were upon its passenger list. When four days out from Southampton, this great ship struck an iceberg in the darkness of the night, and the large and luxurious *Titanic* sank, carrying over fifteen hundred people to a watery grave. While the vessel was steadily sinking and all hope had been given up, the band played Mrs. Adams' inspiring hymn. A Canadian passenger, who was saved in one of the lifeboats, said that as they rowed away, the strains of this comforting hymn came to them from the stricken ship.

During the War Between the States, Bishop Marvin, of the Methodist Episcopal Church, who had been driven from his home, was traveling through a lonely section of Arkansas, much depressed in spirit, when he approached a lonely cabin, having hardly the necessities of life. But from it came the words of the hymn "Nearer, My God, to Thee," sung by its occupant, a poor widow; and the minister's heart was cheered and strengthened.

Two other incidents demonstrate the influence of this hymn in winning wanderers back to the path of righteousness; and also its power to comfort those who already walk in the straight and narrow way.

Years ago, two gamblers sat together at a table, and while one of them shuffled the cards, the other leaned back, and hummed the tune of this hymn. In somewhat startled voice, his companion asked: "Where did you learn that?" "At Sunday school," was the reply. A flood of recollections swept over the soul of the listener. He immediately arose, pushed back his chair, and walked out of the place of temptation to lead a changed life.

On the morning after the earthquake and fire had destroyed a great part of San Francisco, in 1906, a little group that had been made homeless by the catastrophe gathered on a knoll overlooking the blackened ruins of the city, and sang "Nearer, My God, to Thee."

The Sunday School Times of August 10, 1912, contained a number of letters from readers on "A Hymn That Helped Me." Miss Florence Teden, of Brooklyn, New York, wrote: "It was Sunday afternoon. Communion service was held at church, and I, with several young friends, was to partake for the first time. A solemn stillness was over the church. Then suddenly the organ pealed out its music, at first soft and sweet, but gradually increasing in volume, until it rang out loud and clear. Then followed that hymn, so beautiful in its simplicity, but oh, so powerfully appealing to our better, nobler feelings,

> Nearer my God, to Thee,
>   Nearer to Thee!
> E'en though it be a cross
>   That raiseth me.

"I am young, seventeen years old, but the beauty, the solemnity, of the occasion appealed to me. Then, indeed, God seemed very, very near. All through life it will be a precious remembrance—that Sunday afternoon when I first partook of the Lord's Supper, when I gave my promise to be His forevermore."

XV

O HAPPY DAY

During the Moody and Sankey meetings in Great Britain, in 1873, a Christian worker was accosted by a woman, with the words, "O sir, for God's sake, tell me something about Jesus, for I am wretched." "What's the matter?" asked the worker. She replied: "I am lost. Oh, tell me what I must do to be saved!" This woman found Jesus as her Saviour, and that day and her future days were happy in his service.

At the close of the meetings, which had been held in Belfast, Ireland, two notable services were held; one for sinners only, concerned about their souls, and twenty-four hundred came, many of whom found pardon for their sins.

The last service was for those who had been converted during the meetings. There were over two thousand converts present, and a writer thus described the scene: "It was a soul-stirring sight to see that vast multitude, including the Christian workers and ministers, numbering more than three thousand. It was like the sound of many waters to hear this multitude sing the new song. All stood and sang in one burst of praise,

> O happy day that fixed my choice
> On Thee, my Saviour and my God,

The effect was overpowering, filling the soul with the sweet foretaste of the praises of heaven." Truly the redeemed sinner could sing with deep sincerity of the happy day that fixed his choice on Jesus.

Philip Doddridge, the author of this hymn, wrote three hundred seventy-four hymns, not one of which was published during his lifetime. They were carefully written, circulated, and sung from manuscript. Frequently they were "lined out" by the minister. The publication of his hymns came in 1755, four years after the death of the poet.

Mr. Doddridge was the son of an oil merchant in London, England, and was born in that city on July 26, 1702.

He was a member of a large family, being the youngest of twenty children. His parents were earnest Christians, and early directed their son's mind to religious matters. However, they died when he was quite young, but he was fortunate in having loving friends who cared for him. He entered the ministry of the Congregational Church at an early age, and when he was twenty years old, he was ordained, and became pastor of the small congregation of Kibworth.

In 1729, he opened an academy at Northampton for the training of young men for the ministry, and this was his home for over twenty years. Here he accomplished a great deal of literary work. Besides "O Happy Day," among his best known hymns are "Hark! the Glad Sound! the Saviour Comes," and "O God of Bethel." This last hymn was a favorite of Dr. David Livingstone, who carried a copy of it in his journeyings through the wilds of Africa. He would often read aloud,

> O God of Bethel, by whose hand
> Thy people still are fed;
> Who through this weary pilgrimage
> Hast all our fathers led.

It was sung at Dr. Livingstone's burial in Westminster Abbey in April, 1874.

The book by Dr. Doddridge, *The Rise and Progress of Religion in the Soul,* quickly won a prominent and permanent place in religious literature. He is the author of a number of other works.

In a letter to his wife, who was away from home on a visit, he manifested the happiness of his own soul in the fact that his choice was fixed on Jesus. After reciting some of the blessings that had come to him, and the calm and peace that enveloped him, he wrote: "And the reason, the great and sufficient reason is, that I have more of the presence of God with me than I remember ever to have enjoyed in any one month of my life. He enables me to live for Him and to live with Him. It is pleasant to read, pleasant to compose, pleasant to converse with my friends at home; pleasant to visit those abroad —the poor—the sick—pleasant to write letters of necessary business, by which any good can be done; pleasant to go out and preach the Gospel to poor souls, of whom some are thirsty for it, and others dying without it; pleasant in the week-day to think how near another Sabbath is, but, oh, how much more pleasant to think how near Eternity is, and how short the journey through this wilderness, and that it is but a step from earth to heaven."

He was never robust, but the joy of Christian service flooded his life. Finally, the dread malady of consumption fastened itself upon him. He felt that he should seek health in a milder climate, and journeyed to Portugal; but so weakened had become his condition, that soon after he reached Lisbon he passed away on October 26, 1751. He was buried in the foreign cemetery of that city.

The humility of his noble character was expressed to his pupils at Northampton in a discussion of the various ways in which Christians met death. He said: "I wish that my last words may be those of Watts,

> A guilty, weak, and helpless worm,
> On Thy kind arms I fall."

The name of Philip Doddridge is a prominent one in the roster of the great hymn writers of the world.

The hymn, "O Happy Day," was the experience of his own heart.

Many of his hymns, embodying briefly the sentiments of his discourses, were written to be sung immediately after the preaching of these sermons.

Dr. James Hamilton, writing of Dr. Doddridge's hymns in *The British Weekly,* says: "If amber is the gum of fossil trees, fetched up and floated off by the ocean, hymns like these are a spiritual amber. Most of the sermons to which they originally pertained have disappeared forever; but, at once beautiful and buoyant, these sacred strains are destined to carry the devout emotions of Doddridge to every shore where the Master is loved and where his mother tongue is spoken."

The hymn, "O Happy Day," was used as a confirmation hymn in the family of Prince Albert and Queen Victoria.

When William Booth, founder of the Salvation Army, began work as a young man, he would hear this hymn sung more like a dirge than a song of joy. He attended many services where no gladness was expressed in the singing, and where a religious meeting was a somber occasion. This did not satisfy young Booth. The buoyancy of youth was in his heart, and the joy of salvation was also there;

and it was not long before the people realized that his worship of the Lord was a delightsome service.

Many who had found no happy days in the paths of sin have heard the cheerful notes of this hymn sung with glad hearts by the redeemed, and have longed for a joy to which they were strangers. Then through a surrender to Jesus Christ, they found peace, and not only a happy day, but a joyful existence in the Christian life.

Rev. Silas H. Payne, in *Stories of the Great Hymns of the Church*, repeats a story told by the Reverend Duncan Mathieson. Mr. Mathieson went to Dundee, Scotland, during the fair held at that place in order to preach to the crowds upon the streets. During one of his sermons, two young women, on their way to the fair, stopped to listen to the singing of "O Happy Day."

Finally one of the girls said: "Come away, we shall be too late for the fair. Her companion already had become impressed with the spirit of the meeting, and replied: "I dare not go." Her friend left her, and went her way, but she remained to the close of the services, and afterward, she could sing of that very day as the one in which she had fixed her choice on Jesus.

Colonel Nicholas Smith relates the following incident in *Hymns Historically Famous*. It was the regular weekly prayer meeting in the Centenary Methodist Episcopal Church of St. Louis, in 1898. The pastor, Dr. Matthews, was about to dismiss the congregation, but invited anyone who desired the prayers of the church to come forward during the singing of the last hymn.

A well-dressed woman came forward and silently knelt. A thrill of interest ran through the gathering. No one then thought of leaving. Prayers, one after another, were offered with great earnestness. "O Happy Day" was sung from memory and without the organ. When the third verse was sung,

> 'Tis done; the great transaction's done!
> I am my Lord's, and He is mine,

the weeping woman, still on her knees raised her hands in prayer, and made this the happy day of her acceptance of Christ as her Saviour.

The congregation, rejoicing in the conversion of a soul, went out into the stormy night, with peace and gladness flooding their lives, and with the realization that the power of Jesus Christ to redeem the individual was just as great as it had ever been.

In one of his sermons, Charles H. Spurgeon tells the story of his conversion in these words: "We shall never forget the day, some of us, when we left off self-righteousness, and believed in Christ to the salvation of our souls. The marvel was done in a minute, but the change was so great that we can never explain it, or cease to bless the Lord for it.

> Happy day, Happy day,
> When Jesus washed my sins away.

"I recollect the morning when salvation came to me, as I sat in a little Primitive Methodist chapel under the gallery, and the preacher said: 'That young man looks unhappy'; and he added, 'Young man, you will never find peace except you look to Christ'; and he called out, 'Look!' With the voice of thunder he shouted, 'Young man, look! Look now!' I did look. I turned the eye of faith to Jesus at once. My burden disappeared, and my soul was as a bird let loose from her cage, even as it is now as often as I remember the blessed salvation of Jesus Christ."

In *The Story of the China Inland Mission*, by M. Geraldine Guinness, is given an account of a meeting held on shipboard as J. Hudson Taylor and his little company were voyaging to China to take up missionary work in that distant and then little known land. The meeting was held in the forecastle. The sailors and the few passengers on board were grouped around, some seated on sea chests, some on planks, and some standing aloof, as if hesitant about attending the service. At the request of one of the sailors, the little congregation sang "O Happy Day."

In *Bringing in Sheaves*, Dr. A. B. Earle tells the story of Ella Gilkey. The evangelist was holding a meeting in Watertown, Massachusetts, and was staying in the home of the Gilkey family. Ella was a bright and carefree girl. She became converted and found Christ as her Saviour. She rejoiced in her new-found religion. She thought that she had been leading a happy life, but now she realized that worldly pleasure was not to be compared with the joy of Christian experience. She entered heartily into every service of the Master; and those who saw her, apparently in robust health, felt that a long life of usefulness was before her.

In a few days, however, she was stricken ill, and the seriousness of her condition was apparent from the beginning. As the end grew near, she sang her favorite hymn, "O Happy Day." "Yes," she whispered, "it was a happy day." And putting her arm about her heartbroken father's neck, she spoke her last words: "Don't cry for me, Father; Jesus will take care of me."

At a service in China some years ago, as a number of converts were received into the church, this hymn was sung.

Time and again at baptisms, between the baptism of one candidate and the preparation of another for the ordinance, a stanza of this hymn is sung. And what is more appropriate upon such an occasion than the sentiments of these words, "O happy day," expressing joy at entering upon the Christian life.

XVI

FROM GREENLAND'S ICY MOUNTAINS

On his tour around the world, William H. Seward, who was secretary of state under both President Lincoln and President Johnson, visited an orphan asylum in Madras, India. The pupils asked what they might sing for their distinguished guest, and he asked for "From Greenland's Icy Mountains." The children heartily sang this soul-stirring hymn; and well they might, for these orphans were enjoying the inestimable blessings which had come to them through the preaching of the gospel to the remotest nations of the earth. This hymn was written by Bishop Reginald Heber in 1819. He was visiting his father-in-law, Dean Shipley, dean of St. Asaph, and vicar of Wrexham, England. A call had been issued for contributions to the Society for the Propagation of the Gospel, and the dean asked his son-in-law to write a hymn for the occasion.

That young man retired to the other end of the room, and while the older guests were engaged in conversation he composed this hymn. The first three stanzas were written in about twenty minutes, and only one word was changed from the original copy. In the second stanza "heathen" was substituted for "savage."

The hymn was sung in the Wrexham church on the following morning, and it has become a classic in missionary hymnology.

Reginald Heber was born at Malpas, in Cheshire, England, on April 21, 1783. His father, the Reverend Reginald Heber, D.D., was a clergyman of the Church of England, and the boy was surrounded by an environment of cultural and spiritual inspiration.

His elder brother Richard was a great book collector and accumulated a library of one hundred fifty thousand volumes.

Reginald was a precocious child, and could read the Bible when he was five years old, and even as a boy he was a diligent student of its contents. Early in life he manifested the gift for poetry, which afterward gave to him an enduring fame.

He studied at Oxford and won prizes for various literary productions, one of these being his celebrated poem, "Palestine," which he wrote at the age of twenty. Seventeen years after he wrote it he heard it sung at Oxford as an oratorio.

When young Heber first read this poem in Convention Hall at the annual commencement, he was greeted with enthusiastic applause and immediately became the hero of the hour. But the praise showered upon him did not swerve him from the purpose of deep consecration. After the exercises, his parents sought him to shower their congratulations upon him. At first he could not be found, but finally it was discovered that he had gone to his own room, and was upon his knees "breathing out his soul in gratitude and prayer."

Upon leaving college, he entered the ministry, and in 1807 began his work at Hodnet, where he preached for about sixteen years. It was during this period that his great missionary hymn was written. In 1822, he was called to the important pulpit of Lincoln's Inn, London. He did not remain here long, for the next year he was appointed Bishop of Calcutta, and sailed at once to take up his new post of duty and engage in the life of a missionary.

His labors in India were brief, however, as he died unexpectedly on April 3, 1826. He had been busy with his church duties and had become over-heated in that hot climate. He returned home from the services, and in a little while his servant found him in the bathroom, where he had expired from a stroke of apoplexy.

Although he was reared in affluence and security, he never shrank from privation and danger. In 1820, a serious malady broke out in the town in which he was laboring, and without reserve, he gave himself in a personal ministry to the afflicted. When friends remonstrated with him and endeavored to show what a great risk he was incurring, he replied: "I am as much in God's keeping in the sick man's chamber as in my own room." He, however, con-tracted the disease in one of his visits to the inmates of the poorhouse, and very nearly lost his own life through this attack.

With the same zeal, he prosecuted his work in the inhospitable climate of India, and, no doubt, his strenuous activities shortened his days. But brief as was his life, it was lived to a high and noble pur-pose. While he wrote other hymns of distinction, his great missionary hymn is a far more enduring monument than granite or marble could possibly be.

Some of his other hymns are:

> "The Son of God Goes Forth to War,"
>
> "Holy, Holy, Holy," and
>
> "By Cool Siloam's Shady Rill."

The tune to "From Greenland's Icy Mountains" was composed by a young bank clerk, Lowell Mason, of Savannah, Georgia. A lady in the city had received a copy of Mr. Heber's hymn, but she had no music for it. She thought of this young man who, she knew, sometimes wrote music. She sent her son to him to ask him if he would write a tune for it. It is said that the boy returned in half an hour with the composition which, ever since, has been associated with the poem.

Lowell Mason, who afterward became a noted composer of music, was born in Medfield, Massachusetts, on January 8, 1792, and died in Orange, New Jersey, August 11, 1872.

This hymn has stimulated greatly interest in missionary endeavor. Its sentiments, no doubt, have turned the hearts of many to take up work on foreign fields, and have quickened the lives of multitudes to a more faithful support of the great enterprise of foreign missions.

Speaking of her own choir and of this hymn, a writer in *The Sunday School Times* tells of its appeal to the generosity of Christian givers: " 'From Greenland's Icy Mountains,' sung by that choir, with the spirit and the understanding, has drawn a big collection out of the pockets of a congregation not noted for their liberality—to anything foreign: and I think a tune must have reached the soul before it could touch the pocket."

This hymn is a trumpet call to duty. It emphasizes the command of our Lord to his disciples to carry his message to all the world, and it is a hymn to unite our hearts in a common cause.

According to *The Missionary Review of the World*, a missionary society in North Carolina, some years ago, presented a program in which a talk with motion pictures was given, and one of the scenes was the entrance of a choir of young

girls, marching to the strains of "From Greenland's
Icy. Mountains."

It is well for our young people to give especial
heed to this hymn, for in it they may hear a call to

> The joyful sound proclaim,
> 'Till earth's remotest nation
> Has learned Messiah's name.

"From Greenland's Icy Mountains" was sung in
the closing session of the Baptist World Alliance
held in Philadelphia in 1911. To this large gathering had come messengers from distant lands. A
number were from countries to which the gospel
message never had been proclaimed until after the
writing of this great missionary hymn.

When the delegates from America were on their
way to the World Sunday School Convention in
Jerusalem in 1904, they stopped in Athens for a
brief visit and attended a Protestant church in the
city. As the visitors entered, the congregation were
singing "From Greenland's Icy Mountains," and the
Americans joined in the concluding verses which
were sung in Greek.

These travelers were on their way to Palestine,
where our Lord and Saviour gave the message of
his gospel, which was to be wafted in every language around the globe, and which is a message of
salvation for all time.

In 1919, six volunteers, three men and three
women, set out for the Yunnan district to carry to
their fellow countrymen the message of Jesus Christ.
An inspiring "commission service" was held in
Shanghai, and Bishop Heber's words were sung. An
American who was present said that he had been
familiar with this hymn since childhood, but that

never had he been so impressed with it as when he heard this large Chinese congregation singing it with such heartiness.

In 1852, two missionaries went out from the South Carolina Methodist Episcopal Conference to the Pacific coast. As they were pursuing their travels through the Santa Clara Valley, often home-sick and discouraged, they were greatly cheered to hear singing, and they found a man and his wife seated in front of their pioneer tent, singing "From Greenland's Icy Mountains."

During a great revival in Philadelphia in 1858, the United States warship, *North Carolina*, was an-chored in the Delaware River at the navy yard. A number of the sailors on this vessel were converted during this meeting. One day while talking among themselves they learned that they were natives of different countries; and when one of them remarked that he was from Greenland, the little company be-gan to sing "From Greenland's Icy Mountains."

Miss Loy J. Savage, a missionary to China, gave in her report for 1916 to the Foreign Mission Board of the Southern Baptist Convention an account of Bible classes which were held in her mission, which were attended by young boys and old men. She said: "Think of some of these men walking two hundred miles across the country, and back another two hundred miles in order to learn of Jesus."

Then she quoted the stanza,

> Shall we, whose souls are lighted
> With wisdom from on high,
> Shall we, to men benighted,
> The lamp of life deny?

The Reverend T. T. Matthews, who spent many years as a missionary in Madagascar, wanted to sing this hymn at the opening of the new church at a place called Fihaonana. But when he began to sing the tune with which he was familiar, the natives refused to sing. Upon inquiry, they gave as their reason the fact that the tune which he was singing had been used with another hymn; therefore, according to their ideas, it had been married to that hymn and should not be divorced from it. Mr. Matthews, feeling that no hymn was better suited for a dedicatory service in this once benighted land, found another tune suitable for its use, and then the natives sang with enjoyment of spirit and freedom of conscience.

Allan Sutherland says, in *Famous Hymns of the World:* "Someone has well written: 'It does not necessarily take a lifetime to accomplish immortality. A brave act done in a moment, a courageous word spoken at the fitting time, a few lines which can be written on a sheet of paper, may give one a deathless name. Such was the case with Reginald Heber, known far and wide, wherever the Christian religion has penetrated, by his unequaled missionary hymn, "From Greenland's Icy Mountains." '

"Like such well-known hymns as 'Abide With Me,' 'Stand Up, Stand Up for Jesus,' 'Onward, Christian Soldiers,' and others, it was written at a sitting and for temporary need, with no thought of its worldwide usefulness in the coming years."[1]

Mr. Seward, in addition to visiting the orphan asylums in Madras, also attended services at a large church in the city. He has this to say of these exercises: "The beautiful hymn which was sung recalled the memory of Heber, and a fine marble statue in the chancel gave us the classic lineaments of the

---

[1]Copyrighted 1906, and used by special permission.

great Bishop of Calcutta. He it was who was 'zealous for his church, and not forgetful of his station, but remembering it more for the duties than for the honors that were attached to it, and infinitely more zealous for the religious improvement, and for the happiness and spiritual and worldly good of his fellow creatures of every tongue, faith, and complexion.' "

And so this hymn has been sung from Greenland's icy mountains to India's coral strand.

XVII

HOW FIRM A FOUNDATION

When Humbolt, the great scientist, was in South America, the section where he was prosecuting his researches was visited by a severe earthquake. He relates how the trees swayed back and forth, buildings tumbled to the ground, and the earth trembled violently beneath his feet. Destruction was all around him, and then he turned his face toward the skies, and they alone were calm and serene and unmoved.

He was speaking only of the material sky to which he had looked with physical eyes. But the Christian, seemingly overwhelmed by life's calamities, and with every human prop swept away, cannot only look with spiritual vision into the heavenly calm, but with his feet planted firmly upon the solid rock of Christ's salvation, need feel no tremor beneath him, and he can sing that great strengthening hymn, "How Firm a Foundation."

This hymn appeared for the first time in 1787, in *Selections of Hymns From the Best Authors*, compiled by Dr. John Rippon, who was pastor of the New Park Street Baptist Church in London, England. Dr. Rippon succeeded the celebrated commentator, Dr. John Gill, in the pastorate, and was pastor of the church for sixty-three years. Although the location of the church had been changed, this was the church to which Charles H. Spurgeon was called, and where he preached with such marvelous power.

The authorship of this hymn is somewhat uncertain, but it was probably written by George Keith, who was the son-in-law of Dr. Rippon, and also his clerk, and who led the singing in the church for many years.

This hymn has comforted saints of the Lord for generations and has been an inspiration to them in many trying afflictions.

Miss Frances E. Willard, speaking of this hymn in her autobiography, *Glimpses of Fifty Years,* says: "Mother says that at family worship in her home, they were wont to sing together 'How firm a foundation, ye saints of the Lord,' and her parents used to say, 'It would never wear out because it was so full of Scripture.' When mother came back to us after having been confined to her room for six weeks, we sang that hymn for her, Anna and I, at family prayers, and she broke in at the verse about 'hoary hairs,' and said: 'How I enjoyed that for my old grandmother, who lived to be ninety-seven, and then I enjoyed it for my dear father who lived to be eighty-six before he passed away, and my daughter enjoys it for me, who am eighty-four, and perhaps she will live on to be as old as I, when I feel sure she will have friends who will enjoy it just as tenderly for her.'

"I said: 'The hymn is memorable in connection with the St. Louis Convention, where we sang it just before we entered on the great political debate, and I was wonderfully borne up by the words beginning,

> The soul that on Jesus has leaned for repose,
> I will not, I will not desert to its foes.' "[1]

The mother of Lady Henry Somerset presented Miss Willard with a music box, and when the great

[1]Copyrighted by the Woman's Temperance Publication Association, 1889, and used by permission.

temperance worker was asked what music she
would most enjoy, she replied: "The hymns that
mother liked best." And one of them which she selected was "How Firm a Foundation."

The Reverend Charles H. Goote compiled a book,
What Led Me to Christ, in which he gives from
different writers the accounts of their conversions.
In the article written by Miss Willard, she tells of
her own conversion, and of a meeting in the church
of her ancestors, about fifteen miles from Rochester,
New York, at which she dedicated herself fully to
God. Ever since she had begun to make public ad-
dresses, she had wanted to speak in this old stone
church, built by her forefathers in 1815; but the
opportunity did not come until April, 1888.

While visiting her relatives, a meeting was arranged, and the church was packed with relatives
and other admirers. Among the hymns that were
sung was "How Firm a Foundation." Telling of
this meeting, Miss Willard says: "I dedicated myself anew in the 'Old Stone Church' that day to
Christ and to His Gospel, vowing that by His grace
I would be in this and every other world where I
might live a woman whom the Lord could trust."

This great hymn is heard often in conventions and
other meetings of the Lord's people in our own and
other lands. It was sung repeatedly at the Baptist
World Alliance in Philadelphia in 1911, where it
brought comfort to hearts of men and women from
distant countries, where governments had persecuted them for their faith, and who had suffered
time and again for the sake of conscience.

It was one of the favorite hymns at the Student
Volunteer Convention in Des Moines, Iowa, in January, 1920, when over five thousand students from

America and other countries met together for self-examination and dedication to the higher purposes of life.

The American delegates, on their way to the World Sunday School Convention in Jerusalem in 1904, stopped for a few days in Athens. Among the places visited was the site of Paul's great sermon in that ancient city. After reading in concert from the seventeenth chapter of the Acts of the Apostles the account of that notable event, the worshipers joined in singing this appropriate hymn. Dr. Charles Gallaudet Trumbull described this scene in *The Sunday School Times,* and says: "The singing of 'How Firm a Foundation' bore witness to the rock that will outlast the Areopagus."

On Christmas Eve in 1898, the American troops were camped along the hill near Havana, Cuba. Scarcely had the sentinel's call announcing the hour of midnight died away, when from one of the tents arose the familiar strains of this hymn, and a solitary voice rang out "How Firm a Foundation." But the song did not remain a solo, for from tent after tent, other voices joined in, and these words of assurance rolled across the moonlit hills.

On Sunday before Christmas in 1937, the writer heard this hymn coming over the radio from the American Church in Berlin, Germany. Wherever God's people gather together, whatever may be their environment, peaceful or warlike, they may be confident of the firmness of the foundation of the Christian faith.

On March 17, 1939, the WRVA fifty thousand watt radio station was dedicated in Richmond, Virginia. After prayer had been offered by Dr. Ben R. Lacy, president of Union Theological Seminary of

Richmond, this hymn winged its way upon the air waves to listeners near and far, assuring them that every real discovery and achievement of genuine science, directed into proper channels, will bring honor to an all-wise Creator.

Great preparations were made for the meeting of the World Sunday School Convention to be held in Tokyo in October, 1929. A large assembly hall was erected with a seating capacity of twenty-nine hundred. Extensive arrangements were made for the entertainment of delegates from all over the world. Only a few hours before the time set for the opening of the convention, the great hall caught fire, and was quickly reduced to a mass of blackened ruins. This was a distressing occurrence, notwithstanding the fact that there was no loss of life.

That afternoon, in a meeting of the Executive Committee, held immediately following the fire, "How Firm a Foundation" was sung, and especially impressive were the words,

> When thro' fiery trials, thy pathway shall lie,
> My grace, all-sufficient, shall be thy supply.

Standing in front of this building was a beautiful group of statuary with a globe representing the world, and with a missionary, and children of different races grouped around her, with Jesus Christ as the central figure of the scene. When the fire was over, this group was found to be unharmed, not even disfigured by smoke. So we may feel that whatever comes—fires, wars, or rumors of wars—"Nevertheless the foundation of God standeth sure, having this seal, The Lord knoweth them that are his."

Rev. James Gallaher, in the *Western Sketch Book,* gives an account of a visit to General Andrew

(Old Hickory) Jackson at his home, "The Hermitage," near Nashville, Tennessee. Many laurels had been won by this old soldier. Twice had he been honored with the highest office in the gift of the nation, but earthly preferment could not sustain him in the hour of weakness. Mr. Gallaher said: "The old hero was then very frail, and had the appearance of extreme old age; but he was reposing with calmness and confidence on the promise and covenant of God. He had now been a member of the church for several years."

During the visit, General Jackson remarked to his visitor: "There is a beautiful hymn on the subject of the great and precious promises of God to his people. It was the favorite hymn of my dear wife till the day of her death. It commences thus,

How firm a foundation, ye saints of the Lord,

I wish you would sing it now." And the little company sang the entire hymn to the comfort of their host.

In his comments on popular hymns, Dr. C. S. Robinson related this incident in *The Homiletic Review:* "Once in the Oratory at evening devotion, in Princeton Seminary, the elder, Dr. Hodge, then venerable with years and piety, paused as he read this hymn, preparatory to the singing, and in the depth of his emotion was obliged to close his delivery of the final lines with a mere gesture of pathetic and adoring wonder at the matchless grace of God in Christ: 'I'll never—no never—no never—forsake!' "

Colonel Nicholas Smith, in his book, *Hymns Historically Famous,* tells of a meeting that was held a number of years ago in central Kansas, where a

small number had come together for worship. Their
hearts were heavy for they had been discouraged by
the serious failure of their crops that season. The
minister related the story of Miss Fidelia Fiske, of
Shelbourne, Massachusetts, who went as a missionary to Persia, dying in 1864.

The speaker said: "When she was in the Nesto-
rian Mission, in feeble health and much discouraged, she sat on her mat on the chapel floor one
warm, uncomfortable Sunday afternoon, without
support for her weary head or aching back. The
woes of life and her lonely position pressed upon
her like a raging flood, and she was ready to sink
beneath the raging waves, when a woman came
and sat down on the edge of the mat at her back
and whispered to her, 'Lean on me.' Miss Fiske
scarcely heeded the request, and still longed for
support to help her bear the discomfort till the close
of the worship. Presently the words were repeated,
'Lean on me.' Then she divided the weight with
the gentle pleader, but it did not satisfy. In earnest, almost reproachful tones, the voice again
urged, 'If you love me, lean hard.' "

When the minister had concluded his remarks,
and had sat down, an earnest voice began to sing,

> The soul that on Jesus hath leaned for repose,
> I will not, I will not desert to his foes;
> That soul, tho' all hell should endeavor to shake,
> I'll never, no never, no never forsake!

One after another of the worshipers joined in the
song, despair gave way to hope, and when they left
that meeting, it was with a firm conviction that the
Heavenly Father had not forsaken them, and never
would forsake them.

Several verses of this hymn were sung at the funeral of the great philanthropist, Mr. William E. Dodge, in 1883.

An aged minister said that he was accustomed to repeat several hymns before retiring, and among those which he mentioned was "How Firm a Foundation." And this hymn has comforted many saints, as they dropped, not simply into fitful earthly slumber, but into that sleep from which the awakening would come only in the glorious and eternal presence of the Lord.

XVIII

JESUS, LOVER OF MY SOUL

A mighty storm swept the waters of the Atlantic. Mountainous billows followed one another in quick succession; and it seemed that no living or inanimate thing could remain upon the surface of so troubled a sea. However, a ship, a tiny speck upon this great waste of waters, was struggling desperately for existence. It would plunge with terrific force down the side of some great wave, as if determined to dash its prow to pieces upon the bottom of the ocean. But the skilled hand of the helmsman held his vessel to a proper course, and quickly she would be riding the crest of another wave, only to repeat her dangerous maneuver.

All hope of safety was given up by passengers and crew alike; and, as best they could, they resigned themselves to what seemed to be their inevitable fate—a watery grave. But the eye of God was on that vessel and his protection was over it.

Charles Wesley was on this ship, and, although greatly distressed himself, he did what he could to comfort his fellow voyagers. It is said by some that this experience of the storm led him to write the immortal hymn, "Jesus, Lover of My Soul."

However, other experiences are also given as suggesting the hymn. Upon one occasion he was standing by an open window, when a bird, pursued by a hawk, flew into his arms. As he held in safety the little frightened creature, he thought of the buffetings of the human soul, and the dangers to which it is subjected; and he meditated upon the fact that only in Jehovah's presence is there real safety.

Another experience given as that which brought about this composition was the persecution directed against him at Kilalee, County Down, Ireland. Mr. Wesley fled from a mob, who resented his preaching of the gospel, and took refuge in a farmer's milkhouse. The farmer's wife, Mrs. Jane Lowrie Moore, gave the pursuers some refreshments, and secretly opened a back window through which the preacher escaped. He hid under a hedge until the mob had dispersed. No doubt this providential deliverance caused deep thankfulness to fill his heart, and impressed him with the fact that both body and soul needed a sure refuge.

The imagery of the hymn, however, is more suggestive of the storm at sea as its inspiration.

Charles Wesley was the younger brother of John, the distinguished founder of the great Methodist Episcopal Church. He was born at Epworth, England, on December 18, 1708, and lived to the advanced age of eighty, dying in London, on March 29, 1788. He studied at Christ Church, Oxford. He then became associated with his brother in religious work, and accompanied him to America. It was on his return to England that he encountered the great storm mentioned.

Charles Wesley was one of the greatest hymn writers of all time. He wrote about sixty-five hundred hymns, many of which would not be recognized today, even by a literary critic. His reputation for hymn writing does not rest upon the number which he produced, for multitudes of hymns have been written and forgotten, but his fame rests upon a few that have an enduring quality of literary merit and spiritual appeal.

Among his other hymns are:

"O for a Thousand Tongues,"

"Hark! the Herald Angels Sing,"

"Soldiers of Christ, Arise,"

and others. Of course the production that looms above them all, and one that takes pre-eminence in any collection of hymns is "Jesus, Lover of My Soul." It was first published soon after his return from America in 1740, in *Psalms and Spiritual Hymns*. If Mr. Wesley had written nothing else in all his lifetime, this one hymn alone would have won him enduring fame. The singing of Charles Wesley's hymns contributed as much perhaps to the inspiration of the revival, from which came the Methodist Episcopal Church, as did the preaching of his zealous and eloquent brother John.

The hymn, "Jesus, Lover of My Soul" is particularly adapted to all phases of human experience. If one is on the mountain peak of joy, he can sing these words with gladsome voice, or if he is in the valley of despondency, he can sing the same words, although in mournful cadence, and receive comfort from their message.

This hymn is certainly an appropriate one to be sung on shipboard. When Dr. J. Hudson Taylor and his companions were on their way to China to take up missionary work there, where he founded the great China Inland Mission, they often engaged in singing on the vessel, and one of their favorite hymns was "Jesus, Lover of My Soul."

Mrs. John G. Paton, in her *Letters and Sketches from the New Hebrides,* records the experience of a voyage which she had with some fellow missionaries, as they were returning home from a general missionary meeting on one of the islands. They had greatly enjoyed the fellowship together, and now their hearts were saddened at the prospect of separation as they should go to their respective fields of labor.

She says that they were on deck, "enjoying the moonlight until quite late, and having such a musical treat from Mr. Michelson, who sings and accompanies himself on the guitar with such taste. He had been playing it on deck in the afternoon, and we begged him to bring it up again after tea. The moon was brilliantly reflected on the water, and the ship lying so still, when he began with exquisite guitar accompaniment to sing 'Jesus, Lover of My Soul'—the missionaries standing around and joining softly in parts, while we were quietly crying. I have heard oratorios in the old country rendered so that they almost took one out of the body, but never anything that went to my heart like this."

This hymn is a favorite in revival services, and during its singing, many a soul has found refuge in the redemption of our blessed Lord. Silas H. Paine, in *Stories of the Great Hymns of the Church,* tells of a Mrs. Lewis of Norwich, England, who went, a number of years ago, to hear the Reverend Mr. Hook preach. She was in great distress of mind, burdened with a sense of sin, from which she seemed unable to get relief. As she went into the tabernacle, she was almost in despair, but the preacher announced the hymn, "Jesus, Lover of My Soul." The woman was greatly impressed by the words of the song. They were applicable to her own condition, and she felt that someone had informed the minister of her state of mind, and that he had made this hymn for her sake. Through this experience, she was led to accept Jesus as her personal Saviour.

Charles H. Spurgeon relates in his autobiography the following incident of conversion: "Not only has there been a great variety of converts during my ministry, but the means blessed to their conversion have been very varied. One brother, when he came to join the church, told us that, as an ungodly stranger, he was going into Exeter Hall, just as I gave out Charles Wesley's hymn, beginning 'Jesus, Lover of My Soul.' He said to himself, 'Does Jesus really love me? Then why should I live in enmity to Him?' There and then he turned unto the Lord; and, not long after, he came boldly out, and confessed his faith in Christ, and sought to do all he could to lead others to the Saviour."

This hymn has not only brought strength in time of temptation, and exhilaration in periods of spiritual depression, but its use has actually been the means of saving human life.

Some years after the Civil War, an excursion steamer was passing down the Potomac River, and a singer on board was rendering a number of familiar hymns, to the enjoyment and edification of the passengers. As his last song, he sang "Jesus, Lover of My Soul." When he had finished a gentleman stepped up to him and asked: "Beg pardon, stranger, were you actively engaged in the late war?" "Yes, sir," was the reply, "I fought under General Grant."

The questioner then told him that he, himself, had been a soldier in the Confederate Army. He related that eighteen years before, while the terrible fratricidal conflict was being waged, he was ordered one night by his commanding officer, because of the accuracy of his aim, to approach the Federal lines and shoot the sentinel on duty. He crawled stealthily toward the sentry and reached the proper point of vantage. He raised his gun and took aim in the bright moonlight at his victim's heart, and was about to pull the trigger when he heard the soldier singing, and the words,

> Cover my defenseless head,
> With the shadow of Thy wing.

came to him. When he heard these words, he was greatly moved by them, and could not fire; and, although he was disobeying orders, he returned to the Confederate lines, as quietly as he had left them.

The singer, grasping the former Confederate's hand, said that he well remembered that night. He related that when he was put on guard upon that occasion, a feeling of depression overwhelmed him. In distress of mind he paced his beat, and then he lifted up his thoughts to God, and began to sing, and the song was the prayer of his heart. He said, "A great peace came into my soul, and I did not know until today, how God answered my prayer."

Many voyagers, putting out upon the unknown sea, have gone forth, wearing celestial smiles, with the singing of this hymn as the last earthly sound falling upon their ears.

During the Civil War, Tom was a drummer boy whom his comrades, in playfulness, called the "Young Deacon," but they loved him and admired him for his uprightness, and faithfulness to his religious profession. One day, a fierce battle raged, and through it, Tom's drum was heard sounding out the orders of his commander. He fell mortally wounded; but, propping himself against a stump, in his expiring moments, he sang "Jesus, Lover of My Soul." His comrades, wounded and dying upon the field of battle heard and were comforted.

A chaplain bent over a dying soldier and asked if he had any special request to make, and he replied: "Yes, sing 'Jesus, Lover of My Soul.'"

The dying wife of a minister whispered to her husband: "Hide me, O my Saviour, hide me."

On Sunday, August 15, 1875, the great evangelist, Charles G. Finney, lacking only two weeks of completing his eighty-third year, was walking with his wife in the grounds of their home. In the near-by church, of which he had been pastor for many years, the evening service was being held. "Jesus, Lover of My Soul" was sung; and Mr. Finney, standing there in the gathering shadows, joined in the singing of the hymn. That night he was stricken ill, and his spirit passed from earthly scenes at the dawning of the morning.

This was the last hymn sung at the funeral of that other great evangelist, D. L. Moody.

George Duffield, himself, a noted hymn writer, having written the hymn, "Stand up, Stand up for Jesus," paid this tribute in his old age to Wesley's hymn: "One of the most blessed days of my life was when I found, after my harp had long hung on the willows, that I could sing again; that a new song was put in my mouth; and when, ere ever I was aware, I was singing 'Jesus, Lover of My Soul.' If there is anything in Christian experience of joy and sorrow, of affliction and prosperity, of life and death —that hymn is the hymn of the ages."

The great orator and preacher, Henry Ward Beecher, said of this hymn: "I would rather have written that hymn of Wesley's, 'Jesus, Lover of My Soul,' than to have the fame of all the kings that ever sat on earth. It is more glorious, it has more power in it. I would rather be the author of that hymn than to hold the wealth of the richest man in New York. It will go on singing until the trump brings forth the angel band; and then I think it will mount up on some lip to the very presence of God."

XIX

JESUS LOVES ME

A woman missionary doctor sat in a Chinese home, with the family gathered about her, and endeavored to explain to them the Christian belief; and then she sang for them a hymn, "Jesus Loves Me." The missionary was surprised to hear a voice in the courtyard joining in the song. It was one of the servants. She was called in and explained that when she was a patient in a mission hospital, she learned "the Jesus doctrine," and now, given this opportunity, she joined the missionary in teaching it to the household.

This hymn, written especially for children, not only appeals to them and is sung by them with enthusiasm, but it strikes a responsive chord in the hearts of old and young alike. The truth which it expresses, the love of Jesus, is as precious to the gray-haired saint as to the children, who, in their youth are remembering their Creator. It brings the same joy when sung by foreign lips in a strange language as when heard in the native tongue of its American author.

This hymn was composed by Anna Bartlett Warner, and was first published in 1860, in the book, *Say and Seal,* written in collaboration with her sister, Susan Warner.

Miss Warner was born in 1820, at Martlear, New York, on Constitution Island in the Hudson River, not far from West Point. Her older sister, Susan, wrote under the pen name of Elizabeth Wetherell, and Miss Anna's pen name was "Amy Lothrop," but they were known as the "Wetherell sisters," and collaborated in the writing of *The Wide World*, and *Queechy*.

Their home was admirably situated for quiet meditation and literary production. However, they were within easy reach of West Point, the seat of the United States Military Academy, and in this institution they conducted a Bible class for the cadets for nearly forty years. They were regarded almost as members of the faculty of this school. When they died, the funeral of each was held with military honors.

Anna B. Warner died in 1915, her life lacking only five years of covering the span of a century. During their lifetime, her sister seemed to achieve greater literary fame, but this simple hymn, "Jesus Loves Me," will, no doubt, live long after everything else which they wrote has been forgotten, unless it is, perhaps, that other hymn written by Miss Anna, "One More Day's Work for Jesus."

The appeal of the song, "Jesus Loves Me," to the human heart gives it a universal application, and we find it sung around the world. In China, in India, in Japan, and in the depths of the African forest, it rises from the lips of those gathered for the worship of the Lord. Children sing this song in different languages, and in places far distant from one another.

Ruth Winant in *The Sunday School Times*, tells the story of Ah Po, a little Chinese girl. The missionary invited her to come to the mission school, but when the child spoke to her father about it, he replied: "Girls are not fit to be educated; they can never pray for the souls of their parents."

However, yielding to the insistence of his little daughter, he consented for her to attend the school.

On the first day, she heard a song that thrilled her little heart, for it said: "Jesus loves me! this I know, for the Bible tells me so." She wanted to know if Jesus loved little girls as well as little boys; and she was delighted to learn that he did. She went home and told her father about Jesus, the Saviour, who loved little girls, and the heart of this stout man was touched, and tenderness afterward marked his attitude toward his daughters.

Some years ago, Mrs. J. T. Williams, a missionary to China, told in the *Home and Foreign Fields*, of teaching the children to sing "Jesus Loves Me," and in the same issue of the magazine, Mrs. C. K. Dozier, another missionary, told of the enthusiasm with which the Japanese children sang this song.

Mrs. A. L. Shelton, in her life of her husband, *Shelton of Tibet*, gives an account of an exhibition of pony riding and racing held by the natives on one of the mountains. The Shelton family took their tent and, accompanied by the orphan boys under their care, went to the grounds on the previous evening. Before the missionaries retired, the little boys sat in the tent door and sang "Jesus Loves Me"; and their childish voices resounded through the hills of that heathen country.

Dr. George L. Mackay spent many years in Formosa. Oftentimes he visited the head-hunters and was in danger of losing his own head. He tells of a work of grace among the neighbors of these vicious savages, where the hearts of the people turned toward God and where he heard the boys singing joyfully in their own language Miss Warner's hymn.

He speaks of a meeting in a village called Paktau, where a young native evangelist was holding services. The building was crowded, and a number of the people had climbed into the branches of a large tree where they could see and hear. Various converts gave their testimony, and then four native women rose and sang this song telling of the love of Jesus. And well might they sing it, for only through that love could they have peace in their own hearts and security in their land.

A Christian worker in Syria wrote of how joyfully the children sang this hymn, when a Christmas treat, given by a friend in America, was distributed among them.

Dr. Jacob Chamberlain, for many years a missionary to the Hindus, spoke of translating this song into the Telugu language, and then of hearing the children singing it in their native tongue. One day he was riding through a town, when he heard singing coming from a side street. Drawing nearer he saw a little heathen boy with heathen men and women surrounding him singing at the top of his voice "Jesus Loves Me." He heard the people question the boy, and he told them that he had learned the hymn at the missionary school, and that he had also learned about the Bible and about Jesus the Redeemer. "Well," they said, "the song is a nice one. Come sing to us some more." Dr. Chamberlain went on his way thankful for the evangelistic work of this little fellow.

Ella D. MacLaurin related in *The Missionary Review of The World* the story of a Chinese girl in a mission school who heard the pupils sing "Jesus Loves Me," until she resented it. She made her own version, which she sang, "Jesus loves me, but I do not love him." However, under the influence of this Christian school her opposition melted away. She became a devoted follower of the Lord, and joined in great earnestness in singing of the love of Jesus.

Some years ago, a number of Sunday school workers toured some of the countries of the East. In Korea they found thousands, young and old, in the Sunday schools. A great crowd gathered in the old palace grounds at Seoul, and sang in Korean "Jesus Loves Me." And we are told that upon one occasion, the eleven members of the first Protestant church in Japan came together and sang this song over and over again for two hours.

The sentiment of this hymn stirs all Christian hearts, and even its simple language appeals to the old as well as to the young.

The Missionary Review of the World relates a story told by Mrs. George King, wife of the physician who was in charge of the hospital at Lanchowfu, North China. A blind woman had been led to the hospital by her two sons. At first she was greatly afraid of the foreigners, but was amazed when she was told that she would be treated free of charge. Her sight was restored, and it was necessary for her to remain in the hospital only two weeks; yet in that time she committed to memory several passages of Scripture. She realized that it was only through the constraining love of Jesus that the missionaries had come from a far distant land to minister to the needs of her people, and she learned to sing feelingly in her quavering voice Miss Warner's great hymn.

This hymn has comforted many a soul as it passed into the dark valley. Dr. Charles Ernest Scott was called to visit a poor old Chinese one wintry night, and found him rapidly nearing the end of life's journey. When the missionary asked him what he could do for him, the sufferer replied, "Sing 'Jesus Loves Me,'" and the dying man was comforted by these words of song.

Dr. Scott calls this "the favorite hymn of all our Chinese Christians which old men and women seem to be able to learn, even when they can learn no other."

A little Japanese girl, soon after she had begun attending the mission Sunday school, was stricken with a fatal illness, but she had learned several hymns, among them "Jesus Loves Me," and, although upon a bed of suffering, she joyfully day by day sang these songs.

Blind Chang was a Chinese Christian martyred during the Boxer troubles in China in 1900. He had taken refuge in the mountains, where he was safe. But in a distant town fifty Christians were arrested. So great was Chang's influence for the Christian religion, that the Boxers said that they would spare the lives of these fifty if Blind Chang should be delivered to them.

When Chang heard of this offer, he volunteered to leave his place of hiding and asked to be led to the headquarters of the Boxers. He steadfastly refused to give up his Christian faith although he was subjected to torture and the threat of death. Finally, they took him to the place of execution, and he went singing,

> Jesus loves me, He who died,
> Heaven's gate to open wide;
> He will wash away my sin,
> Let his little child come in.

When we hear this song, we should be prompted to an examination of our own hearts, and a new appraisement of daily practices.

We are indebted to *The Sunday School Times* for the report of an address delivered at Northfield by Miss Margaret Slattery. Miss Slattery said: "I lunched in New York with four girls. We talked about relaxation. One girl reads new novels of the most startling kind to relax, and another smokes to relax, and another has some exercise which she takes to relax. They asked me what I did, and I told them I went to sleep; that I thought that is what you were meant to do when tired and needing to relax—you should lie down and go to sleep.

"One of the girls said to me: 'But, Miss Slattery, you believe in self-expression, don't you, the fullest self-expression?'

"I said yes, I did, and if you can express yourself best in a puff of smoke, then puff until you get a better self to express. And when she said it I saw a Wellesley girl on the edge of the swamps of Africa, with a divine light in her face, and twenty little black children at her knees, and I heard them singing, first in English, and then in their own tongue:

Jesus loves me! this I know,
For the Bible tells me so.

"Think of a girl sitting at a table in a New York restaurant expressing herself in smoke, and then of that other girl, young, beautiful, free, who could have anything she wished—her fiance will join her and they will be married in Cairo this fall—think of that girl expressing herself in a group of children who will grow up to remake their nation. That is what I call a type of self-expression that is worthy of the mind, body, and soul of a modern girl."[1]

XX

JUST AS I AM

"That's a subject I don't care to have discussed here this evening."

That is the reply that a young woman is reputed to have made to a minister who spoke to her upon the subject of personal religion. The young woman was Miss Charlotte Elliott, and the minister was the Reverend Cesar Malan, of Geneva, who, at that time, May, 1822, was visiting in England in the home of his friend, Dr. Charles Elliott.

Being interested in the souls of all with whom he came in contact, he was especially solicitous concerning the spiritual welfare of the attractive and accomplished daughter of his friend and host.

"Well," he replied with great sweetness of spirit to this rather curt remark: "I will not persist in speaking of it, but I shall pray that you may give your heart to Christ, and become a useful worker for him."

The entire prayer was answered in a signal manner. The words of the minister smote the heart of the young woman, and drove peace from her mind. She now realized the need of Christ as her personal Saviour, as never before, and also the duty of consecrating her splendid gifts to the service of her Lord.

Two weeks after this she again met the minister, but the coldness of her manner was gone. She welcomed an opportunity to speak to him. She herself introduced the subject of religion. "The question," she said, "you asked me the other evening has abided with me ever since, and caused me very great trouble. I have been trying in vain in all directions to find the Saviour, and I come now to ask you to help me to find him. I am sorry for the way in which I previously spoke to you, and now I come to you for help."

She said that she did not know how to come to Jesus, and her friend replied: "Come to him just as you are."

"But will he receive me just as I am, and now?" she questioned.

"Oh, yes," was the answer, "gladly will he do so."

They knelt in prayer, and Charlotte Elliott laid her gift of song, and all of her other talents upon the altar of her Lord.

The words of Dr. Malan, "Just as you are," were music to her ears, and later, they seem to have inspired the words of that noble hymn,

> Just as I am, without one plea,
> But that Thy blood was shed for me.

Miss Elliott was the daughter of Charles Elliott, and was born at Westwood Lodge, Brighton, England, on March 18, 1789. She was the third daughter of six children. Two of her brothers were ministers of the gospel, and an uncle, the Reverend John Venn, followed this high calling, as, also, did her grandfather, the Reverend Henry Venn, a gifted minister.

Her home was one of piety and culture, and she was afforded excellent opportunities for cultivating her musical and literary talents. In the training of her mental faculties, however, she seems to have neglected the development of her physical strength, and her health became very much impaired in early life, and for many years she was a semi-invalid.

Notwithstanding her ill health, she visited not only various places in England, but also Scotland, Switzerland, Normandy, and other sections of the Continent.

Her father died in 1833, and her mother ten years later, leaving her greatly bereft. Her bereavements fell heavily upon a weakened body, but her heart was strong in her faith in her Lord; and she bore with resignation the afflictions, which at times would be seemingly sufficient to overwhelm her. She felt that the Heavenly Father's care was over her, and that he would never forsake one of his children.

For a number of years she made her residence at Torquay, a celebrated watering place, beautiful for situation, on Tor Bay, about two hundred miles from London; but she eventually returned to Brighton, the place of her birth.

Miss Elliott gave herself to literary work, and hers was a consecrated pen. In 1836, she assumed editorial control of an annual publication, The *Christian Remembrancer*. It is said that in this same year, in the first issue of this publication under her editorial management, the hymn, "Just As I Am," was published anonymously.

Sometime after its publication, a consecrated woman saw it, and, being impressed with its possibilities for good, had a number of copies printed for general distribution. One of these leaflets came into the hands of Miss Elliott's physician, who was himself an earnest Christian. Knowing the devoted life of his patient, and feeling that she would appreciate the sentiments of this poem, he gave her the copy. She was greatly pleased to learn the use which was being made of it; and he was delighted to find out that his friend was its author.

Miss Elliott wrote only about one hundred fifty hymns, but in that number was this undying production, "Just As I Am," which for many years has appeared in almost every hymnbook of note, and which has been translated into many different languages. These few verses have won for her more enduring fame than all her other writings, and, no doubt, have brought to humanity a greater influence for good than many thousands of hymns, which, however meritorious, have been forgotten.

Among her other hymns that endure are:

> "Christian, Seek not yet Repose,"
> "Thy Will Be Done!"
> "My God, Is Any Hour So Sweet," and
> "With Tearful Eyes, I Look Around."

The hymn, "Just As I Am," emphasizes the helplessness of human nature, unaided, to rid itself of evil; but it offers a remedy for sin, efficacious, and free for everyone. It finds man just where he is, broken and robbed upon life's highway, sin-stained, and oppressed by doubt and despair, and holds out to him the offer of forgiveness, and of healing, if he will come to Jesus with a penitent heart just as he is.

Mr. Moody relates the story of a Scotch girl who came into the inquiry room. The minister talked with her, and then said: "Young woman, you go home and read the fifty-third chapter of Isaiah." But the young girl threw up her hands and exclaimed: "I cannot read, I cannot pray. Jesus take me as I am." And that is just the way that Jesus takes us, for it is his blood that cleanses the penitent heart.

Not only does this sentiment appeal to those of humble station, but also to those of exalted position.

A writer in *The Sunday School Times* tells of an occasion in his home when his soul was especially lifted up, and in the depths of the night he sang this hymn. He wrote: "God's promise to pardon, cleanse, relieve, the experience which I knew the author of these words must have had to have been able to write them, together with my own faith and the help of the Holy Spirit, caused these words to be of sweet comfort and uplifting power."

Dr. Alexander Whyte, that great teacher, writer, and preacher of Edinburgh, Scotland, would turn, time and again, from the profound writings of the great thinkers of his own and other days, to the simple words and truth of this hymn.

Queen Alexandra, telling of a great sorrow that had come into her life, says: "In 1888 all my five children received the communion with me, and I gave Eddy (the Duke of Clarence), a little book and wrote in it,

> Nothing in my hand I bring,
> Simply to Thy cross I cling.

and also,

> Just as I am, without one plea,
> But that Thy blood was shed for me,
> . . . .
> O Lamb of God, I come! I come!

"When he died and lay like one sleeping, I turned to the table at his bedside, and I saw the little book in which were written these words; and I could not help feeling that he did cling to the Cross, and that it had all come true."

This hymn is often used in revival meetings because of the wonderful results from its appeal. It has been a favorite of the writer in his own meetings, and he has seen a number profess their Lord while it was being sung.

W. T. Stead, who wrote *Hymns That Have Helped,* and who lost his life when the great ship *Titanic* went down in mid-ocean in April, 1912, said: " 'Just as I Am' is the most familiar formula on the lips of the Christian evangelist in all quarters of the world today."

Dwight L. Moody, one of the greatest evangelists of the world, paid this tribute to this hymn: "It has done the most good to the greatest number, and has reached more lives helpfully than any other hymn."

Dr. Amos R. Wells, for many years editor of the *Christian Endeavor World,* said that perhaps no other hymn ever written had brought so many souls to Christ, and he relates these two instances in *A Treasure of Hymns.*

In 1885, this hymn was sung twice on the same Sunday in The Lennox Road Methodist Church in Brooklyn, New York—first by the young people, and then at the regular service. A few doors away lived a young lawyer, and the windows being open he heard the song each time as it was sung, and it led him to a decision for Christ.

John Wanamaker, one Sunday, told his great Sunday school that a dying youth, who had been present only the week before, had requested that "Just As I Am" be sung on his behalf. And while many voices united in the singing, a visitor to the school was converted.

Mrs. James Earle gives in *The Sunday School Times* an account of a visit which she made to the home of a sick man, who had led a godless life, and whose family were strangers to her. Because of the extreme illness of the patient, and the indifference of his family to spiritual things, a friend requested Mrs. Earle to visit him and talk with him about the salvation of his soul. This she consented to do, provided her visit was acceptable to the household.

She went to the home and thus describes her experience: "As I entered the room where the sick man lay, I saw that he was too ill to talk, or listen to conversation. His eyes were closed, but I stepped to the side of the bed and said very quietly, 'I see you are too weak to speak to me, but I am going to sing to you, and if you follow the words, and say them in your heart, and mean every word, then when I am through singing, Christ will have kept his promise to you, that whosoever cometh to him, he will in no wise cast out, and you will be his forgiven, redeemed child.'

"Then softly, but distinctly, I sang 'Just as I am without one plea.' And on through each verse, until he had heard the full Gospel of Salvation, and its way of acceptance by faith.

"Then I left him, trustingly, but yet not knowing the wonderful work wrought by the Spirit those few moments."[1]

The man recovered, and related how a "sweet singer of Israel," as he called her, had visited his sick room, and sung the message of salvation to him, and that he had accepted it. He joined the Presbyterian church and led a consistent Christian life.

This hymn was sung with great effect at the World Sunday School Convention in Tokyo, Japan, in 1920. After the singing, a number came forward to acknowledge Christ as their Saviour.

---

[1]Copyrighted by *The Sunday School Times*, and used by permission.

Dr. Samuel W. Duffield, in his *English Hymns, Their Authors and History*, tells of a letter which the son-in-law of the poet Wordsworth wrote to Miss Elliott, thanking her for this hymn, and telling her of the joy which it brought to his wife on her dying bed.

The letter reads: "When I first read the hymn, I had no sooner finished than she said: 'That is the very thing for me.' At least ten times that day she asked me to repeat it, and every morning from that day until her decease, nearly two months later, the first thing she asked for was her hymn. 'Now, my hymn,' she would say, and she would often repeat it after me, line for line, in the day and night."[2]

After Miss Elliott's death, which occurred at Brighton on September twenty-second, 1871, over one thousand letters were found among her papers, expressing appreciation of this hymn. No doubt, during her lifetime, thousands of others received a benediction from it, and since then, multitudes have found their way to the Saviour, while its words were sending forth their message.